# BRIDGING THE GAP

The Opportunities and Challenges of International
Priests Ministering in the United States

# BRIDGING THE GAP

The Opportunities and Challenges of International Priests Ministering in the United States

Mary L. Gautier, Melissa A. Cidade,
Paul M. Perl, Mark M. Gray

Our Sunday Visitor Publishing Division
Our Sunday Visitor, Inc.
Huntington, Indiana 46750

ISBN: 978-1-61278-736-7 (Inventory No. T1446)

eISBN: 978-1-61278-337-6

LCCN: 2014938928

Cover design: Tyler Ottinger

Cover art: Shutterstock

Interior design: Amanda Falk

PRINTED IN THE UNITED STATES OF AMERICA

# CONTENTS

# FOREWORD

*Bridging the Gap: International Priests Ministering in the United States* is the outcome of a research study carried out jointly by the Center for Applied Research in the Apostolate and Oblate School of Theology. The Center for Applied Research in the Apostolate (CARA) is a highly respected research institute located at Georgetown University in Washington, D.C. Established in 1964, it conducts social science research and publishes a quarterly bulletin, *The CARA Report*, which tracks sociological data related to the demography of the Catholic Church and its institutions.

Oblate School of Theology (OST), operated by the Missionary Oblates of Mary Immaculate, represents over 100 years of quality theological education in San Antonio, Texas. Its student body brings together seminarians from several dioceses and religious congregations along with lay persons preparing for various ministries. Members of other denominations who wish to pursue degrees in theology are welcomed and integrated into the student body.

OST has been reaching out in a special way to international priests since the year 2000. With the support of a grant from Lilly Endowment Inc., it designed and staffed an *International Priest Internship Program* called the IPI, which continues to this day. The IPI focus is the individual international priest and his challenge of acculturation. In 2008, OST received a second grant from Lilly Endowment Inc. to research and to reflect on the system dimension of the international priest phenomenon.

In this second initiative, called the *International Priest Development Program* (IPDP), various projects are underway including a joint research study with CARA; a review of the accompaniment needs of international priests, particularly in the areas of mentoring and coaching; a special outreach to some dioceses; and the development of an initial framework for an Oblate Institute of Missiology where international priest concerns would be identified and reflected upon in an ongoing way.

The principal components of the CARA/OST research study include an evaluation of the International Priest Internship by program participants, a database of international priests serving in the United States, and an assessment of the situation and needs of international priests and those with whom and to whom they minister throughout the United States. One of the primary purposes of the study is to update and to expand the data currently available and to share it broadly. Some of this research has already been shared in a series of regional reflection events in various locations across the country. The results of these reflection events were integrated into this book.

*International Priests in America,* a book by the late Dean Hoge and Aniedi Okure, O.P., in 2006, is perhaps the most informative publication thus far on the subject. The first sentence of Chapter 1 states, "The Catholic Church in the United States has always had international priests serving in its parishes." Those among us with a bit of vintage well remember the Irish, German, Italian, French, and Polish priests who came to our shores to serve our Catholic population. They served with generosity and significantly influenced our ecclesial culture.

Hoge and Okure titled Chapter 2 of their book "The New International Priest after 1985." It was their way of signaling the new challenge resulting from a shift in the countries of origin of the international priests coming to serve in the U.S. Church. The new international priests are missionaries coming to us in greater numbers from Asia, Africa, and Latin America. They in turn are serving with generosity, and they are also significantly influencing our ecclesial culture. This new challenge must be faced by all involved: the international priests themselves, their pastoral coworkers, and the faithful in the pews.

Beyond the challenges, something historically new is surfacing. Cultural borders are being crossed in ways that profoundly affect both the local and the global. Beyond strategies of reorientation and adaptation, a globalizing Church is emerging within a globalized world. This unfamiliar reality needs to be explored theologically and pastorally, and responded to with the appropriate attitudes and skill development.

Uppermost among the major concerns related to this task is the need to promote greater cross-cultural and multicultural understanding and acceptance. To achieve this understanding and acceptance, a high degree of relational intelligence is called for. This has to do with the ability to enter into another person's worldview with respect and openness. This is of paramount importance for effective leadership in the Church of today and tomorrow. It can help facilitate the prophetic dialogue so needed in our world and in our Church. The international priest can play a unique mediating role in bringing this about.

Oblate School of Theology would like to acknowledge the professional and collaborative way in which the Center for Applied Research in the Apostolate pursued this research study. The project director, Mary Gautier, PhD, was ably assisted by Melissa Cidade, MA, and strongly supported by the executive director, Rev. Thomas Gaunt, S.J., PhD. We thank them all!

Oblate School of Theology is indebted to Lilly Endowment Inc. for its generous funding of the international priest initiatives at OST. Rev. Dr. John R. Wimmer, program director at Lilly, was always a most fraternal source of advice and encouragement. We thank him in a special way!

The Center for Applied Research in the Apostolate and Oblate School of Theology are most grateful to the many international priests who participated in this study and to the various dioceses and institutions that hosted the regional reflection events. Thanks to one and all!

The Center for Applied Research in the Apostolate and Oblate School of Theology express their appreciation to all the bishops of Texas for their willingness to meet with us and to openly share their experience and concerns. In the first of our reflection events, they set a good tone for a fruitful exchange in the several reflection events that would take place in the months ahead. Our fraternal thanks to each of the Texas bishops!

All in all, the research project was a positive experience, and we believe that through it we were able to assess some of the real promise in the present reality of our Church in the United States. May the Spirit help us all bring it to fruition.

As part of the CARA/OST project, the demography of the international priest phenomenon will be monitored with great care over the next five years. The ongoing data will be made available in the quarterly CARA Report.

Rev. Ronald Rolheiser, O.M.I.   Rev. Ronald N. Carignan, O.M.I.
President   Director
Oblate School of Theology   International Priest Development
   Program

# PREFACE

Few contemporary studies exist that explore the phenomenon of international priests serving the Catholic Church in the United States. Anecdotes abound, as do opinions and even some horror stories. And although historical studies give some insight into the conditions that gave rise to large numbers of non-native priests serving in the United States prior to the twentieth century, very little is known about the situation as it exists today. That is the purpose of this book. We incorporate data from a variety of sources—our own research as well as that of others—to help us form this national portrait of international priests serving in the United States.

The Center for Applied Research in the Apostolate (CARA) is a social science research center affiliated with Georgetown University in Washington, D.C. CARA studies Catholic populations and institutions and first studied international priests in 1999 as a small part of a much larger project that was completed for the United States Conference of Catholic Bishops (Froehle et al. 1999). That study included a census of the priest population of all 195 U.S. dioceses and archdioceses in the United States.

One question on that study asked dioceses for the number of international ("foreign-born") priests actively serving in the diocese, either as externs or incardinated in the diocese. Extern priests are priests living outside the jurisdiction of their diocese or religious order, usually for study or some other defined period. They minister at the discretion of the local bishop while they live in his diocese, but the shared expectation is that this is a short-term assignment. By contrast, incardinated priests are those who live and work in the diocese for which they were ordained. Extern priests can become incardinated in another diocese, but only by a process defined in canon law.

The study also asked about the country of origin of these priests. We gave no further definitions or stipulations for the term "foreign-born" and relied on the reported numbers for our analysis. Dioceses reported almost 3,500 foreign-born priests in active ministry, a number that was approximately a tenth the size (11 percent) of all diocesan priests actively serving at that time.

A few years later, the late Professor Dean Hoge of The Catholic University of America was also commissioned to conduct a study of international priests serving in the United States. Dr. Hoge consulted CARA for a definitive estimate of the number of international priests and used an estimate of 16 percent as the basis of his study (Hoge and Okure 2006:11). The book that Hoge and Dominican priest Father Aniedi Okure prepared from their research identifies some of the primary obstacles involved in trying to quantify this phenomenon, such as the reality that this is a very transient population, often serving for just a few years before moving on, and that many of these international priests belong to international religious orders but are sometimes inaccurately counted among the diocesan presbyterate because they are serving in parish ministry.

Subsequent to the Hoge and Okure study, the USCCB Secretariat of Child and Youth Protection began systematically collecting numbers and country of origin data about all international priests serving in U.S. dioceses as part of their annual audits of dioceses. These audits asked dioceses to identify international priests (defined by them as "those priests who were born in and completed priestly formation in a country other than the United States") according to the numbers coming from the ten most common countries of origin as well as a catch-all "other" category. Not all dioceses responded to this question, which was asked in 2008, 2009, 2010, and 2012, but these four time points provide valuable trend data for us, which we use for analyses in Chapter 2.

In 2008, CARA was approached by leaders at Oblate School of Theology (OST) in San Antonio, Texas, about a joint research project on the subject of international priests serving in the United States. CARA and OST set out a comprehensive research plan that included an evaluation of an existing acculturation program for international priests (International Priest Internship, or IPI) that is offered annually by Oblate School of Theology, compilation of a database of international priests serving in the United States, and surveys and focus groups of international priests in the United States as well as those who work with them in pastoral ministry. CARA also conducted a series of focus groups of parishioners at parishes served by international priests. They provided rich detail about their experience, which we share throughout the book.

As a first step in this research for Oblate School of Theology, CARA surveyed international priests who were alumni of the International Priest Internship, to learn more about the process of acculturation and the experiences of priests who had been through such a program. Oblate School of Theology provided contact information for nearly a hundred international priests who had participated in the program between 2003 and 2009. While about a quarter of these priests had already left the United States by the time of the survey (summer 2010), CARA obtained a response from two-thirds of the remaining alumni. This survey, and two focus groups of priests attending the IPI program, provided valuable information about the demographics of international priests coming to the United States to serve, their ministry experience prior to coming, their evaluation of the IPI acculturation program, and their ministry experience since coming to the United States. Some of the findings from this study are also reported here in Chapter 3.

CARA also surveyed diocesan vicars for clergy in 2009, 2010, and 2011 to obtain contact information on international priests in ministry in U.S. dioceses. More than half of all dioceses provided names and addresses for 2,211 international priests, which formed the sampling frame for a survey of international priests. In 2012, CARA mailed a questionnaire to all of these international priests and received a completed survey from 388 priests. A total of 34 surveys were returned as undeliverable, for a response rate of 18 percent (a typical response for a mailed survey with no follow-up). The responses to these surveys form the basis for the discussion of acculturation experiences and formation needs in Chapter 3. The survey responses also provide data for the discussion of ministry satisfaction and challenges in Chapter 5. Where possible, we also compare the responses of these international priests to those of U.S.-born priests from a similar survey of priests CARA conducted for the National Federation of Priests' Councils (Gautier et al. 2012).

To obtain general impressions from the other side of the altar, CARA also included questions about international priests on two national polls of U.S. Catholics. In 2000 and 2008, CARA conducted national polls of adult U.S. Catholics that asked about support or opposition to various approaches to meeting ministry needs of parishes in a time of fewer priests. Among these questions was one about "bringing in a priest from outside the United States." In each poll, more than half of responding Catholics said they would support this as an approach to meeting ministry needs of parishes. They favored this option as much as increasing the use of deacons and asking retired priests to help out more. The only option they favored more highly was sharing a priest with another parish.

CARA then asked those who had experienced an international priest in their parish in the last five years about their satisfaction with his ministry, and more than half said they were "very satisfied" with this ministry. These findings are discussed in more detail in Chapter 4, where we describe the parish experience of international priests. The survey findings are fleshed out by comments from three focus groups of parishioners that CARA conducted in parishes around the country that currently have an international priest serving as their pastor.

Finally, CARA conducted a series of five daylong gatherings of international priests and those who work with them in ministry in five different regions of the country: San Angelo, Texas; Oklahoma City, Oklahoma; Belleville, Illinois; Los Angeles, California; and Washington, D.C. These gatherings brought together about a hundred international priests ministering in the United States, vicars for clergy, immigration personnel, chancery staff, mentoring pastors, and bishops for a daylong conversation about the experience of international priests in ministry in the United States. The insights gained from these five regional gatherings form the basis for our recommendations in Chapter 6.

# CHAPTER 1
## History of International Priests Serving in the United States

I'm at CARA in Washington, D.C., recruiting parishes for a study of international priests. I start by calling parishes and talking with the pastor. A man with a thick accent answers the phone, "Parish rectory. 'Allo?" I converse with the man—who is the pastor of this small, rural parish in Southwest Texas—about the study and ask if he would be willing to recruit a few parishioners for me to interview for this project. He agrees, and we set a date.

A few weeks later, I arrive at the parish for its single Sunday Mass. It's a small, clean building made of aluminum with a corrugated metal roof. There is no stained glass, no statues—it's unlike any Catholic church I have ever seen. Neat rows of dark brown pews face the small altar at the front. The church can hold, at maximum, a hundred people.

I am greeted at the door by a dark-haired woman of about fifty. "*Hola!*" she exclaims. "*Bienvenida!*" She asks me, in Spanish, if I am looking for the *menudo*. I admit to her, in English, that I don't know what *menudo* is. She laughs and answers in English that it is a Mexican soup, and that the parish is selling it by the bowl as a fundraiser. "Why are you here?" she asks. I am getting the idea that they don't get many visitors. As I describe the study and my journey to southwest Texas, parishioners stream in. About nine in ten, by my estimation, are Hispanic—probably of Mexican descent. The rest are Anglo; I would learn later that these families have been long established in this community.

I settle into a pew, careful not to take someone's seat. The music starts, and a tall priest who looks to be from India, with a head of thick black hair and a large, white smile walks down the aisle, singing along to the music in Spanish. My breath catches in my throat: I am surrounded by bilingual Hispanic Catholics being pastored by an Indian priest in far southwest Texas. I'm overwhelmed with the multiculturalism of the situation. I did not know then—as I do know now— how common a scene this is.

Surely, I think to myself, this is some kind of postmodern expression of Catholicism in the twenty- first century. This has to be a new phenomenon, a product of modern globalization. It's only later, after reading, studying, and listening, that I would learn that the history of the American Catholic Church and the history of the international priest are intertwined.

— Melissa Cidade

Who are these men? Why have they come to the United States? And by what means do they come to serve in the United States? The academic literature about foreign-born priests serving in the United States can generally be characterized as addressing one of three topics: the history of international priests in the United States, the current demographic and other descriptive characteristics of these priests, and programmatic suggestions for acculturation and other ways to address problems associated with having an international priest serve at a parish.

This chapter situates the international priest phenomenon in this larger context. First, we discuss briefly the history of this intertwined relationship between Church and priests. Then we present an overview of the literature on international priests, including past research on the topic. Finally, we consider some of the global implications of the international priest from a sociological point of view.

# THE RELATIONSHIP BETWEEN THE CHURCH AND INTERNATIONAL PRIESTS IN THE UNITED STATES

## Foreign-Born Priests and the History of the Catholic Church in the United States

The history of the foreign-born priest in the United States is the history of the Catholic Church in the United States. Before the Revolutionary War, the few Catholic priests in the United States were mostly Jesuits from Europe sent to minister to the small Catholic population in the colonies. As early as 1637, Jesuit priest Jean de Brebeuf sent letters home to France to instruct other Jesuits considering missionary work to the Hurons on proper behavior so as to acculturate to the Huron ways and gain trust and access to them. Brebeuf's instructions varied widely, from the call to have "sincere affection for the Savages" (de Brebeuf 2008:15) to the more specific suggestion, "Be careful not to annoy anyone in the canoe with your hat; it would be better to take your nightcap" (2008:16).

Ferdinand Farmer, a Jesuit priest living in colonial Philadelphia, documented in a letter to a fellow Jesuit that in 1773 the "Catholic religion is tolerated, mainly in Maryland and Pennsylvania" (2008:26), and that the paltry numbers of missionaries, five in Pennsylvania and more in Maryland, served the rural and urban populations of the colonies. In fact, these few missionaries "attend with no mean labor to small congregations of men [sic], nearly all poor and widely scattered," and to the greater "number of souls comprising men [sic] of different nationalities" in the burgeoning urban areas (2008:26).

Another Jesuit priest, John Carroll—who became America's first Catholic bishop—noted the small population of Catholics in his report to the *Propaganda Fide* (now the Congregation for the Propagation of the Faith) in 1785, saying that in Maryland there was 15,800 Catholics, 7,000 in Pennsylvania, about 200 in Virginia, and 1,500 in New York (Carroll 2008:28). Interestingly, Carroll went on to describe that there was a "want of priests" (2008:29), and that the priests serving in the United States are German, Irish, and French Canadians (28-29). In 1791, French Sulpicians, a society of diocesan priests, began arriving. They built the first seminary in the United States, St. Mary's in Baltimore, which is still in operation today. At the first U.S. Church Synod in 1791, 80 percent of the clergy present was foreign-born, mostly from France and Ireland (Hoge and Okure 2006:1).

Beginning in the early to middle part of the nineteenth century, with the advent of industrialization in the United States, waves of immigrant populations, particularly from global Catholic centers, began arriving in the United States. This Catholic influx, concentrated mostly in Irish, Germans, Italians, French Canadians, and Eastern Europeans, including Poles, Lithuanians, and Ukrainians, "transformed the ethnic profile of the United States" (Dolan 1984:135), creating a more ethnically and linguistically diverse Church. Many of these groups immigrated to the United States as communities, and, as such, their community priest often immigrated as well. These clergy came to the United States with the intention of staying here and ministering to their own ethnic population. Thus they were incardinated into the diocesan presbyterate and became a permanent part of the diocese, ministering within the immigrant communities that brought them (Hoge 1987:117-118).

The Irish are an exception to this pattern of immigrant priests coming to the United States to serve their ethnic community. The Irish were overrepresented in both the clergy writ large and the hierarchy specifically. While the Irish were "no more than 50 percent of the Catholic population in 1900 . . . 62 percent of bishops in the United States" at that time were Irish (Dolan 1984:143). In fact, examining the hierarchy in the late nineteenth and early twentieth centuries, author Charles Morris finds that the bishops of the United States were overwhelmingly Irish, but German and French were also represented in the Church hierarchy (Morris 1997:51-52). Throughout the nineteenth and early twentieth century, the majority of clergy were foreign-born; in fact, one study finds that in Minnesota between 1844 and 1880, nine out of ten priests were foreign-born. Of those foreign-born priests, "at least 70 percent . . . were Irish and German" (Dolan 1984:170).

Then, for about twenty years post-World War II, the United States produced enough ordinations for the first time in its history, thus eliminating its dependence on international priests. In fact, during this time period, there were enough ordinations that American priests could go on mission abroad. By 1958, about 6,000 priests, brothers, and sisters were working in the foreign missions (Dolan 1984:393). In fact, the "total number of priests in the United States reached its peak in 1969" (Gautier et al. 2012:1).

## Descriptive Literature on Current Foreign-Born Priests

When foreign-born priests arrived in the United States in the pre-World War II era, their background mostly matched the immigrating populations. As was noted earlier, a sizable proportion of the American presbyterate in the nineteenth and early twentieth centuries were Irish; likewise, a sizable proportion of the American laity in that same period were also Irish. However, those foreign-born priests entering the United States in the late twentieth and early twenty-first centuries are originating from different home countries than the foreign-born priests who came before them. The top sending country for foreign-born priests in the United States in 2012 was India, followed by the Philippines and Nigeria (see Chapter 2). Ireland was in fourth place as a sending country, but most of these Irish priests who came to the United States for ministry did so more than thirty years ago.

Further, unlike earlier waves of foreign-born priests in the United States, recent arrivals often do not stay for an extended period of time and are not ministering to a population similar to the one in their home countries. Hoge finds that non-European priests have difficulty assimilating into U.S. culture and are particularly challenged in ministering in parishes other than those similar to their own background (1987:117-118). In some dioceses, there is a push to match international clergy with parishioners of a similar ethnic background (Smith 2004:11); however, as Americans themselves identify less and less with the immigrants in their family history, this salience may be lost.

The first major comprehensive attempt at documenting contemporary foreign-born priests is Hoge and Okure's *International Priests in America: Challenges and Opportunities.* This book outlines the number of foreign-born priests in the United States, as well as the challenges that these priests experience, based on a 2004 survey of international priests, and eighty-seven interviews and three focus groups with international priests. Several chapters are devoted to the rationale for and against having international priests, as well as some of the impact of these priests on both the sending and receiving dioceses.

In the end, the authors admit that the greater conversation about the inclusion of foreign-born priests is similar to what was said in the early Church in the United States about foreign-born priests from Europe (122). They also make recommendations about the use of international priests, including solving the priest shortage through a series of radical changes in Church teaching, supporting the development of a leadership pipeline in the sending country, orienting priests to the Church in the United States as early as possible, and mentoring international priests during their time in ministry (122-124).

Additionally, newspaper articles occasionally profile the foreign-born priests in a diocese or a parish (for example, Goodstein 2008; Kelly 2012; and others). These articles are generally overviews of the individual priest or priests serving in that diocese or parish and often have little context for the larger phenomenon of foreign-born priests serving in the United States.

## Programmatic and Problematic Literature

A final branch of literature on international priests in the United States outlines programs designed to help international priests to acculturate in the Church here or help parishes adjust to an international priest. These articles are generally published in local or regionalized publications that are specific to priests, religious orders, or those working for the Church.

Acculturation programs usually have to do with training international priests to work within the confines of the Church in the United States. These programs include practical skills, such as accent reduction, and more theoretical information, such as programs on U.S. culture and the Church in the United States. For example, Richard Henning and Sebastian Mahfood (2009) provide an overview of one way of preparing international priests for ministry in the United States through a sort of "Cyber School" for them, using online learning. Roger Schroeder outlines the need for specific skill building around issues of sexuality and gender roles (2009), and Nguyen van Thanh (2011) calls for orientation programs for international priests to include preaching as an element.

Another such suggestion for assisting international priests in acclimating to U.S. culture is the use of mentoring relationships with American and other foreign-born priests and careful attention to the placement of international priests within parishes in the United States (Belford 2008).

Parish-coping programs tend to be mostly about the need for parishes to reach out to the international priest early in the process of coming to the United States. These programs also seek to prepare the parish to accept the international priest. In this case, William Belford suggests that international priests should take the initiative to integrate themselves into the parish community, "whether anyone tells [them] or not, whether [they] are encouraged or not," and they should "consider [themselves] automatically invited and in fact encouraged to get to all clergy meetings and diocesan events and priest funerals" (2008a:31).

This literature, while descriptive of the general history, demographics, and programmatic aspects of international priests, does not address the larger question of the movement of international priests to the United States. How can we think about the migration of this specific set of ministers to America? Why do they come here?

## GLOBAL FORCES: PUSH AND PULL FACTORS

The Catholic Church is a global institution, with more than one billion adherents worldwide; half of all Christians around the world identify as Catholic (Pew Forum on Religion and Public Life 2011:21). As such, it is in constant interaction with other global forces. Using Immanuel Wallerstein's World-Systems Analysis, the Church, and the actors within this global institution, are part of the larger network of economic, political, and social institutions around the globe (2004:16). It must be understood within the context of "social temporalities," particularly with regard to the historical legacy of a 2,000-year-old institution. Within this system, the Church is bound to both the local and the global—the local dioceses and parishes respond to the pressures and norms of the local populace, while the global Church attempts a pan-Catholic identity for its adherents. Some have argued that such an identity is unattainable; that there is always a hegemonic relationship between the European/U.S. Church and the global Southern Church (Budde 1992:21), sometimes referred to as the "third Church" (Bühlmann 1978:21).

The global system shapes the individual actor—or, as Wallerstein describes, individual actors are "not a primordial atomic element, but part of a systemic mix out of which they emerge and upon which they act" (2004:21). Nevertheless, it is the individual priest who migrates to the United States within the larger Church. How are the other global institutions moving these priests around the world? What are the "push" and "pull" factors—the economic and social incentives weighing on the decision to leave the home country—informing this decision to migrate (Massey et al. 1993:433)?

## Pull Factor: Priest Shortage

One of the main reasons that international priests have come to the United States, both historically and in contemporary times, is as a response to the shortage of priestly vocations in the United States. There were chronic shortages of priests during the nineteenth and early twentieth century that eased in the 1940s and the 1950s. These two decades were the only time history saw the U.S. Church well supplied with native-born vocations. In 1969, there were nearly 60,000 priests in the United States. At present, there are fewer than 40,000 total priests, a decline of more than 30 percent.

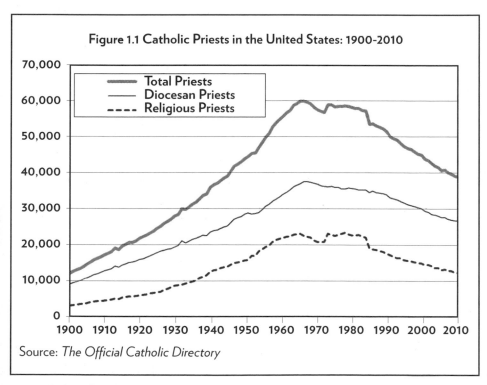

Figure 1.1 Catholic Priests in the United States: 1900-2010

Source: *The Official Catholic Directory*

Much has been written about the priest shortage. As early as the 1980s, sociologists and demographers were writing about the declining number of priestly vocations (Hoge 1987:241). The most widely known of these studies, *Full Pews and Empty Altars* (Schoenherr 1993), used detailed statistical modeling to project the number of active diocesan priests out to 2005. While some have questioned the severity of the priest shortage (Sullins 2002), the number of priests has continued to decline nationally for at least forty years.

At the same time that the number of active priests has declined, the proportion of Americans who are Catholic has stayed roughly the same. Researchers have noted that the Catholic population has remained stable at approximately 23 percent of Americans for almost the entire post–World War II period (Gray 2010). Since the national population is increasing, however, that 23 percent share is equivalent to more people. Indeed, while some argue that the number of Catholics who have left the Church outweighs any increase in population (Putnam 2011), data from the Pew Forum on Religion and Public Life U.S. Religious Landscape Survey (2008) find that while 32 percent of American Catholics "disaffiliate" with the Church, more than two in three (68 percent) remain Catholic.

A long-standing shortage of priests in the United States leads to a "tightened labor market," which may warrant lobbying from Church hierarchy to increase the influx of highly skilled priests to the United States (Karoly and Panis 2009:43). Indeed, several U.S. bishops have been actively recruiting international priests for years (Goodstein 2008). Michael J. Piore argues that "migration seems to respond to the attraction of the industrialized countries" (1979:3), and it reacts to "the search of American employers for new sources of labor" (3). Similarly, if foreign-born priest migration is based more upon the recruitment by industrialized labor markets than the decisions of the priest and the bishops, then it is "the employers, not the workers, and the jobs, not the income, that are strategic" (19).

Recruitment of workers also helps to explain why there are pockets of places that are particularly dependent upon foreign-born priests, and others that seem to have no migrant presence (24). For example, there are 36 dioceses and archdioceses nationally in which 50 percent or more of their presbyterate is foreign-born (Gautier et al. 2012). Others have almost no international priest presence.

## Push Factor: Standard of Living

One of the push factors mentioned with regard to international priests in the United States is an assumption that they are coming to the United States to enjoy a higher standard of living. As Hoge and Okure argue, determining whether or not the priest has come to the United States because of economic motivations can be a challenge, as "a majority of international priests try to hide or deny the economic motivation, and a researcher is seldom able in any one case to say definitely that it is present or how strong it is" (2006:73). They go on to argue, however, that the salary of the priest is a motivator, both in terms of the personal standard of living and the ability to send remittances home to their sending diocese, their parish, and their family (2006:74-75).

The *Instruction on the Sending Abroad and Sojourn of Diocesan Priests from Mission Territories,* published by the Vatican's Congregation for the Evangelization of Peoples, recognizes that foreign-born priests serving abroad can have a focus on economic betterment; the document mentions that "often their motives are based on the higher living conditions which these countries offer and the need for young priests in some of the established Churches" (Tomko 2001). This document reminds diocesan leaders that priests should be sent in a spirit of mission, not in a push for economic betterment.

## Push Factor: Diocesan Leadership

A related push factor for international priests coming to the United States may be the sending dioceses themselves. In many instances, the sending diocese is paid a fee for each of the foreign-born priests who serve in the United States. In some ways, this is perceived as a justice issue; it is, after all, the international diocese that pays to educate and form the priest in the first place. William Easterly and Yaw Nyarko argue that remittances in general (regardless of whether they are to a family or to an institution) "more than cover the cost of educating [a migrant]" (2009:359).

In other ways, this is seen as a commodification of the priest—he becomes a product that is traded by his own diocese to the wealthier receiving diocese.

The full extent of the payment system for international priests is not known; it is in need of further study. Hoge and Okure assume that the practice is "uncommon" (78), but the actual systemization and extent of the change of money for priests is unknown.

Another consequence of the movement of priests between countries is the possibility for "brain drain"—or human capital flight—in the sending countries. All priests, regardless of their country of origin, must complete a rigorous academic and spiritual formation program before ordination. Moving these highly educated men out of the country in which they were ordained could cause detriment to the sending country. Hoge and Okure argue, however, that because the priest needs the permission of the ordinary in his diocese or province, it is unlikely that the impact of this movement will be great (2006:26).

Likewise, the brain-drain analogy is not a perfect fit for international priests because the majority of these priests eventually return to their home diocese. Hoge and Okure place the figure at 50 percent (2006:26), though they admit that this is not a perfect estimate. More likely, international priests, who are usually in the United States on a religious worker visa, are limited to five years in the United States as non-immigrants (GAO Report 1999:3). Not only do most international priests return to their sending dioceses, but they typically do so within five years of coming to the United States.

This lack of permanence has its own consequences. Piore argues that returning migrants are often not well integrated back into the community from which they came (1979:2), finding that it is precisely their high level of education and formation and the expectation of proficiency in English that "weaken the ties that bind the migrants to their home" (1979:118). So, while brain drain may not be an issue due to the temporary nature of international assignments, the international priest returning to his home country may experience reintegration issues (Hoge and Okure 2006:76-77).

## Push Factor: Missionary Spirit

Finally, a major reason international priests cite for coming to the United States is the "missionary thrust" (Tomko 2001) that animates them. Although Piore is not talking about religious workers, he does say that "one can better understand migration by ignoring income differences and recognizing instead that people are rooted in a social context in ways that other commodities are not; migrant behavior can be better understood in terms of the specific attributes of the jobs available to migrants and the meaning attached to those attributes in the social context in which work is performed" (1979:8). Social context—in this case, missionary spirit—is as much an influence on the decision to migrate as money. And, in fact, when most international priests talk about why they have come to the United States, they use the "mission in return" paradigm to frame their decision to serve (Hoge and Okure 2006:71-73; Mabonso Mulemfo 1997:100). It is difficult to measure the sincerity of the missionary spirit. How much of a role does this play in the choice to serve in the United States?

# INTERNATIONAL PRIEST AS A SPECIAL-CASE MIGRANT

The literature about migration is not a perfect fit for understanding the phenomenon of international priests for several reasons. First, international priests typically come to the United States on R-1 visas—religious worker visas. This limits the amount of time they can spend in the country. Also, most migration literature gives the migrant a locus of control that the international priest does not have. Because of his vow of obedience to his bishop or religious superior, the international priest does not necessarily make the decision to migrate to the United States for ministry; neither does he usually decide where to go or how long to stay. Finally, much of the current literature on migration tends to favor family reunification as a major pull factor to migrating workers. However, international priests are not, for the most part, migrating in order to be with family. In most cases, they are leaving their family behind in their country of origin.

# CONCLUSION

All of this, then, begs for further research. What are the motivators of bishops and religious superiors from other countries for sending priests to the United States? And, how do they select which priests will go? What prompts the priest to accept such a position, other than his vow of obedience? What are the larger consequences—theologically and sociologically—of using economic language (i.e., the "importation" of priests) when discussing foreign-born priests? And, how is the Church, as a global institution, interacting with other global institutions in the movement of its clergy? Each of these research questions deserves the time and attention of sociological and economic scholars as the trend toward the globalization of the priesthood seems unlikely to decline in the near future.

# CHAPTER 2

## Contemporary Trends in the Use of International Priests in the United States

My opinion is that most parishioners in American parishes, at least in the Southeastern dioceses, would prefer an Irish priest to an American priest. If this is so, I suspect the reason for it is that the Irish are more pastoral, less bureaucratic, more personal, less rational/academic. Of course, it's quite chic ... to be anti-Irish, but not so among ordinary parishioners. Being thus favored has its disadvantages, however. Some Irish priests play the "Irish ticket" to a shameful degree, *substituting charm for substance. And some Americans are absolutely fixated* on a Barry Fitzgerald/ Bing Crosby "Going My Way" notion of the Irish and nothing one says or does seems to get through to them. I did not come to the U.S. to set up "little Irelands" in my parish!

—Quote from an Irish priest (Smith 2004:86)

As we saw in Chapter 1, the phenomenon of international priests ministering in the United States is quite different now from at any other time in U.S. history. While the number of international priests arriving on U.S. shores continues to grow, they are no longer arriving with the intention of ministering permanently to other Catholic immigrants from their home country. Instead, they more typically come as "missionary priests," invited by a U.S. bishop or sent by their home bishop (or religious superior) for a defined period of time to serve a territory that has too few priests to meet ministry needs. The people that they serve are very different from them, in language as well as culture. The tie that binds them together is their common Catholic faith and a strong desire for the sacraments, which only a priest can provide.

This chapter presents an analysis of available data on international priests serving in dioceses and archdioceses in the United States in order to explore current trends in the distribution of international priests—both where they are coming from and where they are serving. The data we use here come from research conducted by CARA for the United States Conference of Catholic Bishops (USCCB) in 1999, annual diocesan data published in *The Official Catholic Directory*, data reported by dioceses and archdioceses in their annual audits for the USCCB Secretariat of Child and Youth Protection (in 2008, 2009, 2010, and 2012), and data collected from vicars for clergy (in 2009, 2010, and 2011) for this project. We also use statistics about seminarians that CARA collects annually from seminaries in the United States. These data give us trends regarding international priests serving in the United States over approximately the last decade.

## DEMOGRAPHIC TRENDS IN CATHOLIC POPULATION

There are four main trends in Catholic population that are increasing the pressure on U.S. bishops to import priests from outside the United States:

- Steady growth in Catholic population.

- A gradual migration of Catholics from the Rust Belt to the Sun Belt and from the urban core to the suburbs.

- Immigration of Catholics from outside the United States.

- Decreased vocations to priesthood and religious life.

# Growth

The total number of Catholics in the United States continues to grow at a steady pace of approximately 1 to 2 percent per year, as it has since about the middle of the twentieth century. This growth has kept pace with overall population growth in the United States, maintaining the Catholic portion at roughly a quarter of the overall population.

While some have speculated that recent growth in Catholic population is largely due to immigration, particularly Hispanic immigration from Latin America (see Putnam 2010), this is demonstrably not the case. The adult Catholic population born in the United States to native-born parents grew by 24 percent from 1980 to 2011 and continues to make up a majority of the U.S. adult Catholic population (see Fig. 2.1) (Gray 2012). The Catholic population has also increased through immigration and the children of immigrants during this period, but this growth through immigration is not sufficient on its own to increase the overall Catholic population by 1 to 2 percent per year. More interestingly, the percentage of adult Catholics indicating that they were born outside the United States has declined since 2007, and the adult Catholic population percentage has continued to remain stable. This has occurred as immigration rates from Mexico have collapsed (ibid.).

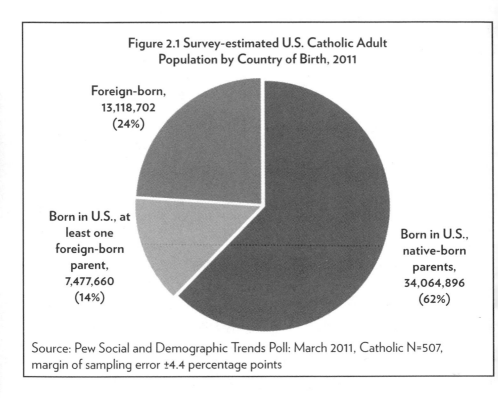

Figure 2.1 Survey-estimated U.S. Catholic Adult Population by Country of Birth, 2011

Foreign-born, 13,118,702 (24%)

Born in U.S., at least one foreign-born parent, 7,477,660 (14%)

Born in U.S., native-born parents, 34,064,896 (62%)

Source: Pew Social and Demographic Trends Poll: March 2011, Catholic N=507, margin of sampling error ±4.4 percentage points

## Migration

Catholics have also been moving out of the traditional ethnic immigrant inner-city neighborhoods of the Northeast and away from the farms and villages in the Midwest that were settled by generations of Catholics before them. Although this had been a gradual process over the course of the latter half of the twentieth century, the effect is now being felt more acutely. For example, in 1950, about three in four Catholics lived in the Northeast (46 percent) and the Midwest (30 percent). Just a little more than half a century later, Catholics are now almost evenly distributed among the four U.S. Census Bureau regions (see Fig. 2.2).

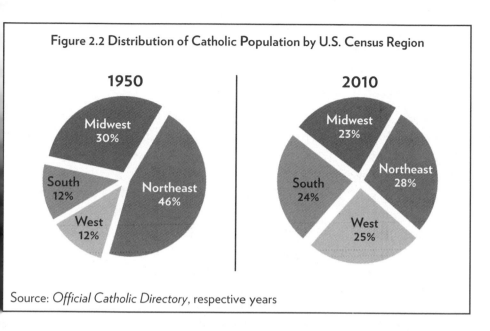

Figure 2.2 Distribution of Catholic Population by U.S. Census Region

**1950**

- Midwest 30%
- South 12%
- West 12%
- Northeast 46%

**2010**

- Midwest 23%
- Northeast 28%
- South 24%
- West 25%

Source: *Official Catholic Directory*, respective years

Just as important as the movement from Northeast and Midwest to South and West, Catholics are also moving from the old urban ethnic neighborhoods and into the suburbs and exurbs surrounding major cities. Immigrant Catholics of the nineteenth and early twentieth centuries settled where they could find employment and community support—typically in the major cities of the Northeast and upper Midwest. They worked hard to provide a better life for their children and grandchildren. As those children and grandchildren gradually assimilated into American society and got a good education (many of them as a result of the GI Bill), they bought houses and raised families in the suburbs, away from the old urban ethnic neighborhoods.

As the Catholic population in the United States gradually migrated away from the traditional centers of Catholic life the resulting impact on Catholic institutions has been noticeable. Dioceses and archdioceses in the Northeast and upper Midwest are shuttering schools and parishes, while those in the South and West struggle to finance and build parishes large enough to accommodate rapidly growing Catholic populations. Parishes and schools in the inner cities find it difficult to attract enough Catholics to remain open and viable, while parishes in the suburbs add extra Masses and suburban Catholic schools maintain long waiting lists.

## Catholic Immigration

Along with the internal movement of the U.S.-born Catholic population, more recent immigrants from traditionally Catholic countries continue to add to the number of Catholics in the United States. More than 12 percent of the U.S. population is foreign-born, according to the U.S. Census Bureau, and Asia and Latin America are the two world regions that have the greatest number of immigrants to the United States (U.S. Census 2010). Large numbers of Catholic immigrants from the Philippines, Vietnam, and southern India, as well as immigrants from predominantly Catholic Latin America, have swelled the Catholic population, particularly in the West and Southwest.

The map here displays the overall Hispanic population in the United States according to the 2010 U.S. Census and shows the dioceses, mostly in the Southwest, in which a sizable proportion of the overall population is Hispanic. Although not all Hispanics are Catholic, research indicates that more than half, and in some cases as many as two in three, self-identify as Catholic (Perl et al. 2006).

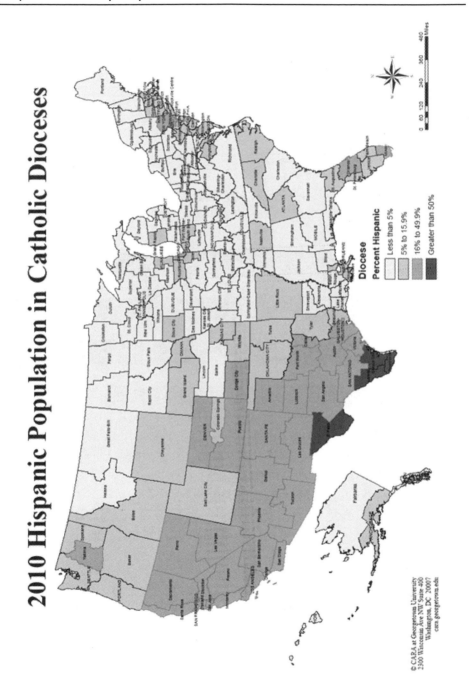

2010 Hispanic Population in Catholic Dioceses

Diocese
Percent Hispanic
Less than 5%
5% to 15.9%
16% to 49.9%
Greater than 50%

© CARA at Georgetown University
2300 Wisconsin Ave NW Suite 400
Washington, DC 20007
cara.georgetown.edu

0  60  120    240    360    480 Miles

This immigration has increased the multicultural complexity of Catholics in the United States, particularly young Catholics. As figure 2.3 shows, each generation of Catholics is more diverse in terms of race and ethnicity than the one preceding it. The younger two generations are now more than half of all adult Catholics in the United States, and their diversity presents special challenges for the Church.

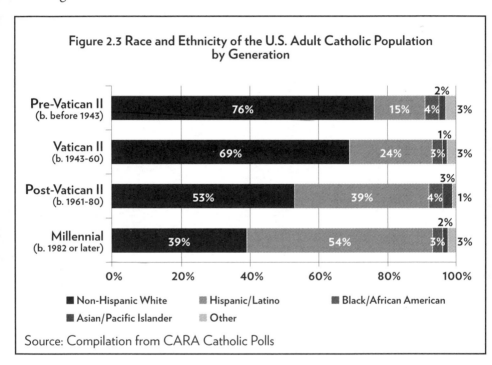

Figure 2.3 Race and Ethnicity of the U.S. Adult Catholic Population by Generation

## Priests

The final demographic trend that is increasing the demand for priests from outside the United States to minister to this growing Catholic population is a declining number of available U.S.-born clergy. The total number of priests in the United States peaked in 1969, while the total Catholic population living in the United States continues to grow approximately 1 to 2 percent per year (Gautier et al. 2012). Consequently, the overall number of Catholics per priest, which was at a relatively manageable 800 or less throughout the first half of the twentieth century, began increasing rapidly in the early 1980s and is now well over 1,700 Catholics per priest (see Fig. 2.4). If we exclude retired priests from this equation, the number of Catholics per priest in 2012 is more like 2,500 to one.

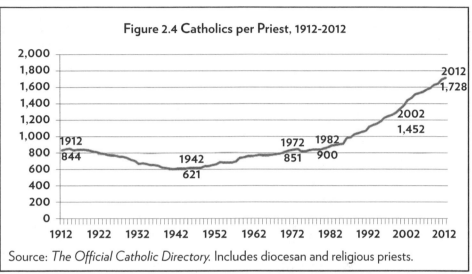

Figure 2.4 Catholics per Priest, 1912-2012

Source: *The Official Catholic Directory.* Includes diocesan and religious priests.

The reasons why there are fewer priests now than there were in 1969 are fairly straightforward—the large numbers of men ordained in the 1950s and '60s, who are now retiring or even dying, are being replaced by much smaller ordination cohorts. Two factors combine to increase the number of priests: 1) ordination of men to the priesthood in the United States, and 2) the importation of priests from outside the United States. The total number of priests is diminished in size when priests die, retire from active ministry, or depart for some other reason. The net decline in the number of priests is explained by the differential effects of these two forces: priests are retiring and dying at a faster rate than that of ordinations and importations.

In 1970, there were about 58,000 total priests (diocesan and religious) in the United States, their average age was 35 and fewer than 10 percent of them were over the age of 65. By 2009 there were about 41,000 priests overall, with an average age of 63 and more than 40 percent were over the age of 65 (Gautier et al. 2012).

Ordinations to priesthood peaked in the late 1960s at just over 1,500 per year and have declined to around 450 to 500 per year in the last twenty years. In 2012, there were 457 men ordained to the priesthood in the United States, of whom about 350 were diocesan priests and about 100 were ordained for a U.S.-based religious order (*The Official Catholic Directory* 2013). At this time, there are only about one-third as many incoming new priests as are necessary to replace those priests who are dying or otherwise leaving active ministry. In fact, a recent CARA survey of diocesan priests revealed that half of those currently active (in 2009) expect to retire before 2019 (Gautier and Bendyna 2009). Many may continue at some reduced level of active ministry during retirement, though.

In 1970, only 3 percent of priests were retired and 97 percent were in active ministry. By 2009, 78 percent of priests were in active ministry, 7 percent were semi-retired, and 15 percent fully retired (Gautier et al. 2012). In fact, the graying of the priesthood is the one trend that is perhaps having the most immediate impact on priestly life in the United States.

This aging and diminishing presbyterate, combined with a growing and increasingly diverse Catholic population, has encouraged many bishops to welcome international priests to serve in the United States (see Fig. 2.5).

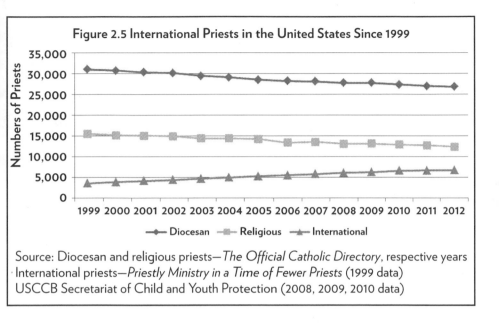

Figure 2.5 International Priests in the United States Since 1999

Source: Diocesan and religious priests—*The Official Catholic Directory*, respective years
International priests—*Priestly Ministry in a Time of Fewer Priests* (1999 data)
USCCB Secretariat of Child and Youth Protection (2008, 2009, 2010 data)

# WHAT IS AN INTERNATIONAL PRIEST?

What is an international priest? For the purposes of this study, an international priest is a priest who was born outside the United States, received his priestly formation outside the United States, and was ordained for a non-U.S. diocese or a religious order based outside the United States. In canon law terms, these priests are incardinated[1] in a diocese or a religious institute outside the United States and serve here as externs, on a short-term or temporary basis.

In reality, however, the situation is much more cloudy and difficult to determine with any level of precision. We know that many, if not most, of the international priests who came with the European immigrant Catholics of earlier generations arrived in the United States with the intention of staying here and ministering to the members of their ethnic community on

---

[1] Canon 265: Every cleric must be incardinated into some particular church or personal prelature or into an institute of consecrated life or society endowed with this faculty, so that unattached or transient clerics are not allowed at all. (Canon Law Society of America 1983)

a permanent basis. They were received into the dioceses where they settled and were incardinated into the local presbyterate by the bishop. The same was true of the large numbers of Irish priests who came to the United States with the Irish immigration beginning in the 1830s. The Church in Ireland had an abundance of priests in the nineteenth century, and the bishops there sent thousands of them as missionaries to English-speaking countries around the world.

> By the mid-1800s, 59 percent of the priests in the diocese of New York were Irish-born and at the beginning of the twentieth, 62 percent of the bishops were Irish-American, more than half of them being Irish-born. By 1900, two-thirds of the diocesan priests in the Diocese of St. Paul, Minnesota, were foreign-born with more than one-quarter of them being Irish. One-third of the pastors in the Archdiocese of San Francisco in 1963 were born and educated in Ireland, while during the 1940s and 1950s, 80 percent of the priests in the Archdiocese of Los Angeles were Irish-born. (Smith 2004:14)

These Irish priests settled in, were incardinated, and became an accepted and valued member of the clergy of their respective dioceses. Because they were sent as missionaries to the United States they were expected to minister to all ethnic groups, not just the Irish immigrants that were here. Their local bishop regularly placed them in parishes of other ethnic Catholics, such as Slovaks, Bohemians, Italians, Polish, and Portuguese (Morris 1997). In this regard, they are similar to the international priests arriving in the United States in modern times—the priests coming to the United States to serve nowadays are expected to speak English and to be validly ordained clergy in good standing, but there is no expectation that they will be matched in terms of ethnicity or culture with the people they will serve. They come to the

United States on a temporary visa[2] with an average of more than ten years' ministry experience in their home country (Cidade and Gautier 2010) but too often with little or no preparation for the culture they will encounter once they get here. Their adjustment to American parish life is sometimes rocky; they may feel marginalized from other priests in the diocese and typically have little or no opportunity to socialize and share experiences with other international priests. Each of these challenges will be discussed in more detail in later chapters.

Just identifying international priests is challenging. *The Official Catholic Directory*, which is the most authoritative census of Church personnel in the United States, does not identify priests by nationality.[3] In most contemporary cases, international priests will be classified as extern priests, because they serve in the United States under the authorization of the local U.S. bishop in the diocese where they reside (as we described above), but they are here only for a period of time and remain incardinated in the diocese from which they came. Their intent, and the expectation of their bishop, is to return to their home diocese after a term in the United States.

Not all externs, though, are international. Externs may also include priests from another U.S. diocese on special assignment, priests who are pursuing higher education in a diocese other than their own, and other scenarios. International priests who wish to stay in the United States and have legal permanent residency (or U.S. citizenship) are incardinated in a U.S. diocese and are counted as diocesan priests, not externs. Finally, religious order priests are another special case—even if they are members of a non-U.S.-based international order but are serving with faculties in a parish or other sponsored work of their religious order, the diocese typically lists them as a

---

[2] Most international priests now arrive in the United States on an R-1 (religious worker) visa, which allows them a maximum stay of five years.

[3] The statistical listing of ministry personnel by diocese in *The Official Catholic Directory* presents several categories of diocesan priests (active in the diocese, active outside the diocese, serving in foreign missions, retired/sick/absent), religious priests serving in the diocese, and extern priests serving in the diocese. None of these are identified by country of origin, however, and foreign-born are found in all categories.

religious priest rather than an extern. *The Official Catholic Directory*, then, provides little guidance in understanding trends in international priests serving in the United States.

## COUNTRY OF ORIGIN OF INTERNATIONAL PRIESTS

CARA conducted the first ever national census of international priests serving in U.S. dioceses and U.S.-based religious institutes for the U.S. Conference of Catholic Bishops in 1999 (Froehle et al. 1999). Based on that census, CARA estimated that about 3,500 foreign-born priests were serving in parish or diocesan ministry in the United States, approximately a tenth as many international priests as total incardinated diocesan priests. In 1999, about a quarter of those foreign-born priests were externs, less than one would expect to see today. In that census, however, incardinated Irish priests were the largest group of international priests, followed by priests from India, the Philippines, Poland, Mexico, and Vietnam.

Dean Hoge, a sociologist at The Catholic University of America, also tried to obtain an accurate estimate of the number of international priests in the United States. He surveyed all U.S. dioceses and the 100 largest institutes of men religious in 2004 to obtain lists of priests born overseas whose ministry in the United States began in 1985 or later (Hoge and Okure 2006:11). Extrapolating from the places that responded to his request, he estimated roughly 5,500 international priests in 2004, approximately 4,500 of them were diocesan priests, and the rest were priests from religious orders (or about one international priest for every seven incardinated diocesan priests). Because he asked only for men serving in 1985 or later, he effectively excluded nearly all the Irish-born priests who are incardinated in dioceses. He did not try to estimate the proportion of international priests of different nationalities, although a fifth of his sample was from Latin America and another fifth was from India (Hoge and Okure 2006:153).

Finally, the most accurate counts of international priests serving in dioceses at this time have been achieved by the U.S. Conference of Catholic Bishops in the annual audits mandated by the Charter for the Protection of Children and Young People and conducted by the Secretariat of Child and Youth Protection. In 2008, 2009, 2010, and again in 2012, the auditors asked dioceses to tally the number of international priests serving in each diocese and to identify them by country of origin. Although not every diocese complied with this request in every year, the numbers are accurate enough to provide some reasonable estimates and to explore trends. And although the auditors asked dioceses for this information only, it is evident from the explanations supplied by dioceses along with their data that more than a few dioceses went beyond the original request and also included international religious order priests in their counts.

In 1999, international priests made up 8 percent of all priests serving in dioceses in the United States, and there was approximately one international priest for every ten diocesan priests. By 2012, the USCCB reported more than 6,600 international priests, which represented 17 percent of all priests in the United States.[4] There is now approximately one international priest for every four incardinated diocesan priests in ministry in the United States (see Table 2.1).

---

[4] The data used for calculating international priests as a ratio of all diocesan and religious priests are from *The Official Catholic Directory*, respective years. The publication year for OCD corresponds to the previous calendar year (i.e., the 2012 OCD reports data collected in 2011) and all data reported here exclude Puerto Rico, Guam, and the U.S. territories. The 1999 data on the numbers of international priests are from Froehle et al. The 2008, 2009, 2010, and 2012 data on the numbers of international priests are from USCCB Secretariat of Child and Youth Protection audit reports, respective years, with missing data interpolated from surrounding years.

| Table 2.1 Top Sending Countries, by Year | | | | | |
|---|---|---|---|---|---|
| **Sending Country** | **1999** | **2008** | **2009** | **2010** | **2012** |
| India | 342 | 825 | 865 | 830 | 972 |
| Philippines | 327 | 706 | 687 | 686 | 702 |
| Nigeria | 101 | 522 | 565 | 566 | 616 |
| Ireland | 827 | 732 | 703 | 715 | 599 |
| Mexico | 224 | 473 | 426 | 496 | 505 |
| Poland | 256 | 346 | 396 | 428 | 455 |
| Vietnam | 231 | 354 | 299 | 342 | 366 |
| Colombia | 143 | 296 | 309 | 342 | 344 |
| Spain | 117 | 158 | 162 | 181 | 163 |
| Sri Lanka | 49 | 43 | 54 | 54 | 36 |
| Other | 874 | 1,518 | 1,673 | 1,803 | 1,859 |
| **Year Total** | **3,491** | **5,973** | **6,139** | **6,543** | **6,617** |
| International as a percentage of total incardinated priests | 8% | 15% | 15% | 16% | 17% |
| International as a percentage of all diocesan priests | 11% | 22% | 22% | 24% | 25% |

Source: USCCB *Priestly Ministry in a Time of Fewer Priests* (1999 data)
International Priests, USCCB Secretariat of Child and Youth Protection

In 1999, the largest group of international priests was from Ireland, many of whom arrived in the first half of the twentieth century to serve in mission dioceses in the South and the West, where the rapidly growing U.S. Catholic population was underserved by U.S.-born priests. These Irish priests have been retiring from ministry and declining in numbers; by 2012, there were fewer than 600 of them and they were the fourth largest group of international priests serving in the United States. The largest group of international priests is now from India, close to 1,000 in all. In addition to the Irish priests, more than 500 priests each from the Philippines, Nigeria, and Mexico also serve in the United States. Other major sending countries include Poland, Vietnam, Colombia, and Spain.

## Table 2.2 Top Receiving Arch/Dioceses in 2012 (Numbers of priests from each sending country)

| | India | Philippines | Nigeria | Ireland | Mexico | Poland | Vietnam | Colombia | Spain | Other Countries | Total 2012 | Total 1999 | Change 1999-2012 |
|---|---|---|---|---|---|---|---|---|---|---|---|---|---|
| Los Angeles | 25 | 51 | 18 | 80 | 59 | 11 | 24 | 7 | 19 | 126 | 420 | 331 | 27% |
| New York | 62 | 38 | 58 | 6 | 8 | 12 | 1 | 6 | 16 | 104 | 311 | 235 | 32% |
| Galveston-Houston | 18 | 27 | 20 | 3 | 15 | 5 | 48 | 5 | 7 | 47 | 195 | 56 | 248% |
| Newark | 21 | 37 | 15 | | | 20 | 1 | 11 | | 26 | 131 | 175 | -25% |
| San Bernardino | 4 | 21 | 19 | 12 | 23 | 2 | 13 | 1 | 5 | 20 | 120 | 13 | 828% |
| Atlanta | 10 | 6 | 2 | 18 | 9 | 3 | 11 | 27 | 2 | 29 | 117 | 26 | 350% |
| Rockville Centre | 19 | 7 | 31 | 2 | 1 | 12 | 1 | 10 | 2 | 30 | 115 | 47 | 145% |
| San Jose | 6 | 25 | 1 | 10 | 9 | 3 | 27 | 2 | | 32 | 115 | 40 | 188% |
| Orlando | 4 | 10 | 2 | 30 | 3 | 6 | 4 | 17 | 3 | 32 | 111 | 53 | 109% |
| Miami | 7 | 2 | 7 | 37 | 4 | 4 | 1 | 4 | 8 | 30 | 104 | -- | -- |
| San Francisco | 4 | 45 | 5 | 7 | 11 | 1 | 3 | 1 | | 25 | 102 | 65 | 57% |
| Phoenix | 3 | 15 | 9 | 15 | 13 | 3 | 4 | 4 | 3 | 30 | 99 | 27 | 267% |
| Chicago | 8 | 2 | 13 | 1 | 7 | 11 | 4 | 3 | | 48 | 97 | 90 | 8% |
| New Orleans | 2 | 7 | 6 | 14 | 1 | | 36 | 2 | 2 | 27 | 97 | 74 | 31% |
| Oakland | 22 | 10 | 4 | 8 | 4 | 4 | 3 | 5 | | 36 | 96 | 24 | 300% |
| Denver | 4 | 1 | 4 | 5 | 18 | 9 | 9 | 3 | 13 | 24 | 90 | 12 | 650% |
| San Antonio | 1 | 5 | 3 | 12 | 14 | 24 | 1 | 4 | 3 | 23 | 90 | 85 | 6% |
| Austin | 9 | 5 | 14 | 8 | 13 | 2 | 5 | 8 | 2 | 21 | 87 | 8 | 988% |
| Brooklyn | 7 | 10 | 19 | 2 | 1 | 6 | | 7 | | 35 | 87 | 68 | 28% |
| St. Petersburg | 13 | 9 | | 21 | 1 | 9 | 3 | 3 | 5 | 22 | 86 | 34 | 153% |
| Metuchen | 17 | 12 | 1 | 9 | | 27 | | 2 | 8 | 7 | 83 | 37 | 124% |
| Palm Beach | 3 | 1 | 1 | 25 | 1 | 3 | 6 | 5 | 2 | 32 | 79 | -- | -- |
| Corpus Christi | 30 | | | 14 | 1 | 8 | 6 | 7 | 5 | 5 | 76 | 26 | 192% |
| Paterson | | 2 | 3 | 15 | | 17 | | 17 | | 19 | 76 | 53 | 43% |
| San Diego | 1 | 40 | 3 | 8 | 4 | 2 | 3 | 2 | 5 | 12 | 75 | 51 | 47% |

Source: USCCB *Priestly Ministry in a Time of Fewer Priests* (1999 data)
International Priests, USCCB Secretariat of Child and Youth Protection (2012 data)

# RECEIVING DIOCESES

International priests are serving across the country in dioceses and archdioceses large and small—both in terms of their geographic area and the size of their Catholic population. Table 2.2 presents the U.S. dioceses that had at least seventy-five international priests in their ranks in 2012 as well as the countries from which these men have been sent. It also displays the total number of international priests each of these dioceses reported in 1999 and a final column shows the percentage change in the number of international priests in each of these dioceses between 1999 and 2012. It may be interesting to note that Miami and Palm Beach reported no international priests in 1999 and that the number of international priests has decreased in only one diocese (Newark) between 1999 and 2012.

The Archdiocese of Los Angeles reports the greatest number of international priests in 2012, just as it did in 1999. The total number of international priests serving in Los Angeles increased by 27 percent between 1999 and 2012. Other dioceses reporting at least 100 international priests in 2012 included the Archdioceses of New York, Galveston-Houston, Newark, Atlanta, Miami, and San Francisco, as well as the Dioceses of San Bernardino, Rockville Centre, San Jose, and Orlando: eleven in all.

Some dioceses that had few international priests in 1999 report very rapid growth in the number of international priests in the last decade. The Diocese of Austin reported eight international priests in 1999; by 2012 they reported eighty-seven, a tenfold increase in a little more than ten years. The Diocese of San Bernardino similarly reports an eightfold increase, the Archdiocese of Denver reports a sixfold increase, and Seattle, Atlanta, and Oakland each report more than a threefold increase. Other dioceses that more than doubled their number of international priests between 1999 and 2012 include the Archdiocese of Galveston-Houston as well as the Dioceses of Phoenix, Honolulu, Corpus Christi, San Jose, St. Petersburg, Rockville Centre, Metuchen, and Orlando.

Due to the way the data on international priests were reported by dioceses in their audits, it is impossible to tell with certainty how many of these priests are diocesan or religious, or whether they are incardinated or externs. Forty dioceses report a total number of international priests that is proportionally half or more of their total diocesan presbyterate. In fact, three dioceses report a total number of international priests that exceeds their total number of diocesan priests. It is likely that many dioceses are including international priests from religious orders in the international priest totals that they report in their audits. When compared with the total number of priests (diocesan and religious) in the diocese, just eleven dioceses report that half or more of their total presbyterate are international priests.[5] These include the Dioceses of San Bernardino, Honolulu, Stockton, Tyler, Orlando, Palm Beach, Baker, Laredo, Reno, Biloxi, and Amarillo. Sixty-five dioceses report that at least a quarter of their total presbyterate are international priests.

This begs the question of why some dioceses have relatively high numbers of international priests while other dioceses have few or none. Surely the shortage of available U.S.-born priests must be a factor: five of the dioceses that have more than 100 international priests also have a ratio of more than 2,500 Catholics for each active incardinated priest in the diocese. But the addition of international priests brings only one of these dioceses (Galveston-Houston) to a more favorable ratio of approximately 2,000 Catholics per priest. International priests in Atlanta improve the ratio there to about 2,500 Catholics per priest, but the addition of more than 100 international priests in Rockville Centre, San Bernardino, and Los Angeles still means they have more than 3,000 Catholics for every priest. And why do some dioceses with relatively high Catholics per priest ratios still have very few international priests? Dioceses such as Orange, El Paso, Fort Worth, Dallas, Fresno, Brownsville, and Las Vegas each have at least 5,000 Catholics per priest—even

---

[5] Another five Eastern-rite Churches report that a majority of their priests are international, but these eparchies are churches with their origins in Eastern Europe, Asia, and Africa that minister to a predominantly immigrant Catholic population. Their situation is more similar to the immigrant European Catholics of the nineteenth century who brought their native clergy with them to America.

when you include their international priests—yet each of them has fifty or fewer international priests.

It seems that the greater distances between Catholics in some dioceses with fewer Catholics spread out across many miles may also be a factor: Texas dioceses such as Tyler, Amarillo, and San Angelo cover vast territories with a relatively sparse Catholic population (10 percent or less). Each has about half as many international priests as it does total incardinated priests. Baker, in Oregon, and Biloxi, Mississippi, are similar cases. Catholics make up less than 10 percent of the total population in these largely rural areas that cover more than half of each state. Each diocese has more than half as many international priests as it does total incardinated priests, and this gives them a very comfortable ratio of about 500 Catholics per priest. Other dioceses in which the Catholic population is also very dispersed, however, such as Helena, Great Falls-Billings, Fairbanks, Anchorage, and Cheyenne, have very few incardinated priests but also very few international priests.

A third factor might be the attraction of a desirable climate: Miami, St. Petersburg, Palm Beach, Orlando, Venice, and Honolulu each have more than fifty international priests despite having a ratio of 2,500 Catholics per incardinated priest or less, even before factoring in international priests. The two northern Florida dioceses also have more than thirty international priests despite a Catholic population of less than 10 percent.

The reputation of a world-class city could be another factor: New York, Los Angeles, San Francisco, Chicago, and New Orleans attract many international priests because they are international cities with large ethnic populations. Each of these have about a hundred or more international priests. This factor also benefits some neighboring dioceses, such as Newark and Rockville Centre on the outskirts of New York, San Bernardino next to Los Angeles, and San Jose outside of San Francisco. Each of these neighboring dioceses also have more than a hundred international priests. Yet there are other neighboring dioceses, such as Brooklyn (neighboring New York), Orange (neighboring Los Angeles), and Sacramento (neighboring San Francisco) that have few international priests.

A final factor seems to be the presence of a large ethnic population. This is certainly the case for the large urban dioceses described above. It is also the case for the eparchies of the Eastern-rite Churches, as described in footnote 5. More than half of these eparchies report sizable numbers of international priests, many of whom are priests from their respective homelands, brought in to minister to their largely immigrant population. Other dioceses with relatively large Hispanic immigrant populations, such as Corpus Christi, Brownsville, Laredo, and El Paso in Texas, as well as Tucson and Phoenix in Arizona, also have a sizable proportion of international priests.

The patterns are interesting and complex. None of these factors alone can explain why some dioceses have many international priests and others only a few. All of these factors together explain only part of the variation. Ultimately, the determining factor is the decision of the bishop. If the bishop and his advisers want to accept international priests, then he will make it happen. As one bishop described to us in a focus group:

> I "inherited" Indian priests that had come from one particular diocese. That has been a plus, because the priests helped me with their local bishop in trying to screen priests for our area. When the priests have been involved with that, who are serving in our diocese, we have had really good priests. (Gautier and Gaunt 2012)

## THE SPECIAL CASE OF INTERNATIONAL SEMINARIANS

A number of bishops also sponsor international seminarians who are preparing for priesthood in U.S. seminaries. CARA collects annual enrollment data from forty-one U.S. theologates, including one in Rome and one in Mexico, that are supported by the U.S. bishops. Since 2000, CARA has collected data on the number of international seminarians studying in these seminaries as well as their country of origin. These data indicate that approximately a quarter of the seminarians enrolled in these theologates each year are foreign-born, and this proportion has been very stable over those years.

In 2012-2013, the 879 international seminarians reported to be studying for priesthood in these theologates (26 percent of all seminarians in U.S. theologates) come from eighty-one different countries. Six in ten are preparing for ordination for a diocese in the United States, and another one-fifth are preparing for ordination for a U.S.-based religious order. The remaining one-fifth are studying in the United States but plan to be ordained to a diocese or religious order outside the United States. The greatest numbers of these international seminarians are from Mexico, Vietnam, Colombia, the Philippines, Poland, and Nigeria (Gautier 2013:18).

There are some obvious advantages for dioceses that are sponsoring the formation of international seminarians at U.S. seminaries. These men receive their priestly formation alongside the U.S.-born classmates that they will serve with after ordination. They are acculturated into the language and customs of U.S. Catholics, which makes it far easier for them to adapt to U.S. parish life after they are ordained. It also helps them to integrate more fully into the presbyterate of the diocese in which they will serve. One bishop described for us the advantage he sees in having men from other countries receive their priestly formation in U.S. seminaries:

> The seminarians we have who are international—if
> we have at least a couple of years with them [in U.S.
> seminaries] it seems to be the most productive. Those
> are the ones who seem to integrate. And I can see
> it right away when we have gatherings of priests,
> how they mingle or intermingle with the rest of the
> presbyterate. (Gautier and Gaunt 2012)

# CONCLUSION

Four main trends in Catholic population have placed increased pressure on diocesan bishops in recent years to bring in priests from outside the United States. These trends include a steady growth in the number of Catholics in the United States, the gradual migration of Catholics out of the cities and across the United States, an increasing stream of Catholic immigration from other world regions that also have large numbers of Catholics, and a declining number of available U.S.-born clergy. The convergence of these trends has resulted in more than 6,500 international priests coming into the United States to serve in pastoral ministry. These priests serve in nearly every U.S. diocese, although no clear pattern emerges to explain why some dioceses employ many international priests while others do not. Finally, some U.S. bishops are sponsoring international seminarians in U.S. seminaries as another way to address the shortfall in vocations.

Who are these international priests serving in the United States? Chapter 3 considers this question in more depth, exploring their characteristics and describing their experiences of acculturation in the United States.

# CHAPTER 3
# Characteristics of International Priests and Acculturation in the United States

We had one priest who landed here and didn't speak a word of English. Thank God the cabdrivers were from Nigeria, because they spoke the language he spoke, and he got to our parish. Nobody knew when he was coming.

—Nigerian priest in a midwestern diocese

Who are the international priests serving in U.S. parishes these days? Where do they come from? What is their experience prior to their ministry here? How prepared are they for the challenges that they face when they arrive? To begin to address these questions from a national perspective, we compared the characteristics of the priests we surveyed who were alumni of the International Priest Internship at Oblate School of Theology in San Antonio as well as the priests who responded to our national survey of international priests serving in the United States in 2012.

## BACKGROUND CHARACTERISTICS

One-fifth of international priests responding to CARA's 2012 national survey (20 percent) have entered the United States since 2006. The survey finds that the majority of international priests were ordained for a diocese; 69 percent are diocesan priests (see Table 3.1), and 31 percent are religious priests, nearly identical to the ratio of diocesan to religious for all priests in the United States, 68 and 32 percent, respectively (Gautier et al. 2012:xii). However, international priests are younger, on average, than their American-born counterparts, especially those who have entered the United States in recent years. Nationally, the average age of Catholic priests overall is 63 (Gautier et al. 2012:3). For international priests, the average age is 53, and for those international priests who have entered the United States since 2006, the average age is 45.

International priests are not inexperienced, however. On average, international priests have been ordained for twenty-five years. Those who entered the United States since 2006 have been ordained, on average, for sixteen years. Most international priests (78 percent) are involved in parish ministry.

| Table 3.1 Overview of International Priests, by Year of Entering the United States | | | |
|---|---|---|---|
| | Overall | Before 2006 | Since 2006 |
| Percentage diocesan | 69% | 68% | 72% |
| Average years since entering the U.S. | 15 | 19 | 4 |
| Average age | 53 | 56 | 45 |
| Average years since ordination | 25 | 28 | 16 |
| Percentage in ministry in a parish | 78 | 80 | 73 |
| Source: CARA's 2012 national survey of international priests | | | |

What are the motivations these priests have for coming to the United States? Almost three in four (73 percent) say that a desire for ministry in the United States describes why they have come to the United States either "somewhat" or "very well." Almost half indicate that the request of a U.S. archbishop, bishop, or their religious superior describes "somewhat" or "very well" why they are currently ministering in the United States. Other relatively important motivations include the request of a religious superior and the desire to pursue educational goals (see Table 3.2 for more information).[6] One thing that appears to have changed over time is the importance of requests from bishops in international priests' home countries. Just 11 percent of priests who came to the United States prior to 1980 describe such a request as being a "very" influential reason for undertaking ministry here. This compares to 40 percent of priests who have arrived since 2006.

| Table 3.2 *How well do the following describe your reasons for undertaking ministry in the United States?* (Percentage giving each response) | | |
|---|---|---|
| | "Somewhat" or "Very well" | "Very well" Only |
| Desire for ministry in the United States | 73% | 49% |
| Request of a U.S. arch/bishop | 49 | 38 |
| Request of my religious superior | 44 | 37 |
| Desire to pursue my educational goals | 41 | 24 |
| Request of my arch/bishop from home | 32 | 21 |
| Need to support my family/community | 19 | 8 |
| Source: CARA's 2012 national survey of international priests | | |

# PARTICIPATION IN ACCULTURATION PROGRAMS

So far, this book has outlined the historical and current trend of international priests in the United States, especially the change in the numbers of such priests serving in ministry. The men come from various countries and serve in different ministries, but what they have in common is their shared experience of being "international"—that is, they are not from the United States. This "otherness" can cause cultural and linguistic mismatches; one way to bridge

---

[6] The first column in Table 3.2 presents the *combined* percentage for "somewhat" and "very well." Thus the percentage in the second column is *contained within* that of the first.

the divide is through the use of acculturation programs, or programs designed to introduce the international priest to U.S. culture.

The U.S. bishops urge that pastoral ministers (including priests, but also women religious, brothers, and lay leaders of the Church) who arrive from abroad to serve in this country receive orientation to help them adjust to U.S. culture:

> The process of sending and receiving pastoral ministers and their striving to adjust to a new culture while beginning pastoral ministry often generate stressful situations for both the pastoral ministers and their host communities.
>
> These situations have arisen, in part, due to (a) lack of orientation of the pastoral ministers to American society and church; (b) failure to attend to the cultural differences between the host communities and those of the pastoral ministers; (c) false perceptions by both the pastoral ministers and their host communities; (d) assumptions by the host communities that, because the pastoral ministers are Catholic, they will automatically be at home with the Church in the United States....
>
> The need for orientation of the missionary to the local church and society, and an understanding of the cultural contexts, are vital for effective ministry, both for the minister and the community to which he or she ministers. (USCCB, "Guidelines for Receiving Pastoral Ministers in the United States," 2003:3)

Generally, the struggles of acculturation for international priests come in two overlapping forms: issues adjusting to U.S. culture and issues adjusting to the Catholic Church in the United States. The process of adjusting to American cultural expectations is more acute for those coming from nations without a shared language (unlike those from Ireland, Canada, or the United Kingdom, who have little difficulty adjusting to American English). This is also true for ecclesial differences. Chapter 4 in this book outlines the cultural mismatches that sometimes present themselves in parish settings.

Given these cultural mismatches, how prevalent is participation in formal orientation or acculturation programs among international priests in the United States? Approximately half (49 percent) of international priests responding to CARA's 2012 survey said that they had participated in such a program. Among those who *have* participated, about seven in ten have participated in a program run by their own diocese or religious order. About six in ten have participated in a regional or national program.[7] (Many international priests have participated in *both* kinds of programs.) An interesting finding is that among those who have participated in an acculturation program of some sort, many did not do so immediately after arriving in this country. In fact, two-fifths did not participate until having been in the United States for at least a year. Later in this chapter we share the thoughts of some international priests about the ideal timing of acculturation programs.

Table 3.3 shows the overall rate of participation in an acculturation program by various background characteristics. Not surprisingly, relatively few priests born in Ireland, the United Kingdom, or Canada have participated in an acculturation program (just 5 percent). Aside from the cultural similarities that their countries share with the United States, these priests have served in this country for a disproportionately longer time than those from many other parts of the world. Many were well accustomed to life and ministry in the United States before acculturation programs started to become relatively common (roughly in the 1990s). The participation rate is higher among priests born in other European countries and in Latin America—though at 24 and 43 percent, respectively, which is still below the overall average. The rate

---

[7] Examples of such regional or national programs include the International Priest Internship at Oblate School of Theology in San Antonio; the Acculturation Program for International Priests at the Vincentian Center for Church and Society, St. John's University, New York; and the Cultural Orientation Program for International Ministers (COPIM), Loyola Marymount University, Los Angeles.

is highest among priests born in Asia or the Pacific Islands and in Africa (55 and 58 percent, respectively).

---

**Table 3.3** *Have you ever participated in an orientation or acculturation program designed specifically for international priests to serve in the United States?*

(Percentage responding "yes")

| | |
|---|---|
| All International Priests | 49% |
| Diocesan | 50% |
| Religious | 45 |
| **Place of Birth** | |
| Ireland, the United Kingdom, Canada | 5% |
| Europe (other than Ireland and the UK) | 24 |
| Latin America | 43 |
| Asia or Pacific Islands | 55 |
| Africa | 58 |
| **Ordination Cohort** | |
| Pre-Vatican II and Vatican II (ordained prior to 1977) | 22% |
| Post-Vatican II (1978 to 1991) | 53 |
| Millennial (1992 to 2005) | 56 |
| Benedict XVI (2006 to present) | 57 |

Source: CARA's 2012 national survey of international priests

---

Table 3.3 also shows that priests of the Pre-Vatican II and Vatican II ordination cohorts—those ordained prior to 1977—are considerably less likely than priests ordained more recently to have participated in an acculturation program, as we would expect. Priests from the more recent ordination cohorts, from those of the Post–Vatican II (1978-1991) cohort to those of the Benedict XVI cohort (2006-2012), are more likely to have attended an acculturation program. Of course, ordination cohort provides an imperfect picture of how participation has increased over time. Table 3.4 provides a clearer view, breaking down participation by the year priests entered the United States. The second column shows that there has been a steady increase over time in the proportion of priests who have participated in an acculturation program within one year of arriving in this country, from none of the respondents who arrived prior to 1970, to 46 percent of those who arrived after 2005.[8]

**Table 3.4 Participation in an Orientation or Acculturation Program, by Year of Entry into the U.S.**

(Percentage who have participated; the first column is the sum of the latter two)

| Year Entered the U.S. | Total | Participated Within a Year of Arrival | Participated More than a Year After |
|---|---|---|---|
| Before 1970* | 11% | 0% | 11% |
| 1970s | 22 | 11 | 11 |
| 1980s | 50 | 15 | 35 |
| 1990s | 43 | 23 | 20 |
| 2000 to 2005 | 64 | 37 | 27 |
| 2006 to 2011 | 51 | 46 | 5 |

Source: CARA's 2012 national survey of international priests
*There is a very small sample size (9) for this category.

## MINISTERIAL AND FORMATION NEEDS

Next, we turn to the ministerial and formation needs of international priests. In what areas do they feel most prepared for ministry in the United States? In what areas do they feel least prepared? Table 3.5 shows the extent to which international priests report being prepared for ministry in several areas. Results are broken down by the length of time the priests have been in the United States. Overall, almost half of international priests (48 percent) say that they feel "very well" prepared for ministry with people preparing for Catholic marriage. About one in three (36 percent) are "very well" prepared for pastoring more than one parish and for mentoring an international priest

---

[8] Not shown in the table is that—among those who *have* participated within a year of arrival—there has not been much change in recent decades in the likelihood that they have participated within *one month* of arrival. The proportion has stayed roughly constant at around three-tenths of these priests.

for U.S. ministry. Fewer international priests evaluate themselves as "very well" prepared for the multicultural aspects of American parish life, however. About one in four (24 percent) say they are "very well" prepared for ministering in bilingual or multilingual parishes and for ministry with youth ages 12 to 18. The smallest proportion of international priests say that they are "very well" prepared for ministry with Spanish-speaking Catholics; just one in five (22 percent) describe themselves as "very well" prepared for ministry with this group.

| Table 3.5 *How prepared are you for ministry in these settings?* (Percentage responding "very well") | Overall | Time Ministering in the U.S. | |
|---|---|---|---|
| | | Five Years or Less | More than Five Years |
| People preparing for Catholic marriage | 48% | 31% | 53% |
| Pastoring more than one parish | 36 | 38 | 36 |
| Mentoring an international priest for U.S. ministry | 36 | 23 | 38 |
| Bilingual or multilingual parishes | 24 | 22 | 24 |
| Youth ages 12 to 18 | 24 | 15 | 26 |
| Spanish-speaking Catholics | 22 | 15 | 23 |

Source: CARA's 2012 national survey of international priests

There are two significant differences in Table 3.5 based on the length of time priests have been in the United States. Those who have been in the country for more than five years are more likely than their recently arrived counterparts to report being "very well" prepared for ministry with people preparing for Catholic marriage, suggesting that this kind of ministry may be learned, in part, "on the job." Perhaps not surprisingly they are also significantly more likely to feel prepared to mentor another international priest. Notice that those who have been in the United States for over five years are *not* more likely to say that they feel "very well" prepared for pastoring multiple parishes. This may be a reflection of the arrangements of parishes in many parts of the globe, where more than one worship site is not unusual.

## PRIESTS' REFLECTIONS ON ACCULTURATION TRAINING AND MINISTRY PREPAREDNESS

Qualitatively, what do priests say about their preparedness for U.S. ministry and the acculturation programs designed to help them in this area? In five focus groups of international priests conducted around the country, priests discussed these issues with us.[9] In some cases, the international priests feel that that acculturation programs are not as effective as they could be. The training programs can be disorienting to a newly arrived priest, particularly if they involve his moving to another location before he has the opportunity to settle into his new parish. The timing of acculturation programming varies widely. For some, such programming is conducted in the early part of their tenure in the United States; for others, a period of adjustment is given before any kind of formal programming begins. Still others mentioned that there was no formal or informal training for them once they were assigned to the United States.

A few priests mentioned that there was little to no support for him upon entering the United States. One priest ministering in a midwestern diocese described his entry to the United States and mentioned that "from day one, I started working." Another told the story we see at the opening of this chapter—the Nigerian priest who arrived in the United States speaking no English, was not met at the airport, but made it to his new parish because the cab driver happened to be from Nigeria and spoke his language. While not quite as jarring, another priest mentioned that his entry to the United States began with a "priest who received me at the airport and I stayed the night with the vicar for clergy." However, "the next day was meetings all day, and the following day I celebrated Mass."

---

[9] See Chapter 6 for a description of these gatherings.

Several international priests mentioned that the acculturation programs offered to them take place in a very short period of time. One such priest ministering in southwest Texas described the programs as preparing the priests "so we can use them very quickly" and said the programs "don't take enough time to share with [the international priests] and teach them." Another international priest serving on the West Coast echoed this sentiment, pointing out that the international priest is brought to the United States in order to be placed in ministry, and that this urgency can lead to issues with acculturation programs:

> The [local, university-based] program was a longer program, but the pastors and bishops said they cannot release the men [to participate for so long]. So they developed a more intense schedule. The ideal [kind of priest] they are trying to work with is the person who has been here long enough to know the "nuts and bolts," but has questions about why do people in the United States think certain ways. By focusing on what is culture and how every culture has its pluses and minuses, they have tried . . . to offer something that would be helpful.

Another priest outlined that in his midwestern diocese "the orientation is staying at the bishop's residence" and "spending some time in different parishes in the area and concelebrating Masses," along with "an introduction to the diocesan offices." He went on to say that "one of our priests has brought up the idea of an orientation program, but there is an issue of cost or time frame," questioning, "if [an orientation program requires] several months that they would be away, is it really the best use of time to have someone in a program?"

Those who go through such programming shortly after entering the United States find it to be helpful. One priest, ministering in the southern United States, described spending time at an abbey within the receiving diocese with another international priest before placement, and that this arrangement "had an advantage because [the two priests] spoke the same language and [the receiving priest] understood the society we came from and had lived [in the United States] for some time, so he knew what the transition looked like." This priest went on to describe the well-developed program of receiving international priests in the diocese:

> The diocese has developed an organized system of receiving new priests and helping them to serve in the diocese. They have introduced a mentorship program. They have identified twenty priests in the diocese. When you come in, you are received by a priest from your home country. After three or four weeks, you are assigned to a mentor. It is a pre-assignment program. He takes you through the steps of running the parish. Now our brothers who are coming in, they are given a mentor whose duty is to help them to adjust and to understand what needs to be done in the parish. After six months, he is assigned to a parish.

> At the diocesan administration center, before a priest is assigned to a mentor, there is a day that they bring the new priest to the diocese to show him around the offices. Staff members come and talk to him; they make sure he is aware of the help he can get from different offices, especially financial, which is crucial. They tell you what they expect from you in the parish. They tell you about the benefits. If a new priest comes in and is assigned to a parish without the expectations explained, the pastor will tell him what the pastor thinks is expected; but this way, they get it directly, firsthand.

# PRIESTS' RECOMMENDATIONS FOR IMPROVED MINISTRY PREPARATION

In a national survey of priests who have participated in the International Priest Internship Program (IPI) at Oblate School of Theology (OST) in San Antonio, participants were asked the question, "Now that you have more experience as an international priest in the United States, how could IPI have better contributed to your preparation for your ministry?" Three general suggestions emerged in response: first, the program should focus on practical issues of running an American parish; second, the program should be held at a particular moment in an international priest's ministry in the United States (although opinions varied as to the optimal timing for an acculturation program); third, acculturation programs like IPI should include an opportunity for ongoing cultural formation.

Regarding practicality, one respondent said that these programs should be "not just theory but practical experience . . . with a tutor or teacher." Another suggested that the program, "instead of teaching so much theology, concentrate on parish practical pastoral ministry." One asked for "some idea of parish council meetings, procedures. . . . Financial matters are completely neglected, and we do not know about budgeting, accounting and financial matters" at parishes in the United States. He went on to add that these financial issues are "very necessary."

International priests also need orientation on a practical level to the groups within a parish, including linguistic and cultural minorities and others. Said one, "At the time, they did not address liturgy in African-American or Hispanic communities." Another mentioned the need for "an awareness of cultural diversity" and an "emphasis on Spanish language," as well as more on working with "lay leaders, and especially women," while a third respondent called for "more input about Hispanic culture."

There was some disagreement in the timing of when an international priest should attend an acculturation program like IPI. Some said it should be as early as possible, with one saying it is analogous to fueling up before driving a car. Another echoed this sentiment, saying that "a priest must attend [the program] as he begins his ministry." Others disagreed. One respondent suggested that the program "would have been more profitable if I had joined it after two years in this country."

## PERCEIVED HELPFULNESS OF VARIOUS CONTINUING FORMATION AREAS

Using the data collected by the national survey of international priests, a clearer picture begins to emerge about what is needed in acculturation programs. Respondents were asked how helpful several continuing formation-program topics would have been when they first began ministry in the United States. Seven in ten respondents (69 percent) say that learning about the culture of U.S. Catholics would have been "very helpful." Between three-fifths and two-thirds say that formation on the following topics would have been "very helpful": the culture of the United States generally, parish administration and finances, U.S. pronunciation, and the history and ecclesiology of the Catholic Church in the United States—all issues that are mentioned by international priests as areas of friction in their ministry (see Chapter 4 for more on this).

Other topics are less likely to be described as potentially having been "very helpful" for priests when they first began ministry. For example, slightly more than one-third (36 percent) say that language study other than English early in their ministry placement would have been "very helpful." And fewer than half say that training related to working with certain special populations within the parish—including youth ministry, working with women, and working with permanent deacons—would have been "very helpful." It may be that respondents would want a more general introduction to U.S. culture early in their ministry placement, or it may be that only international priests who regularly interact with these groups would want continuing formation about them. See Table 3.6 for more data.

## Table 3.6 *How helpful would continuing formation in these areas be/have been...*
(Percentage responding "very helpful")

| | at the time you first began ministry in the U.S.? | in your ministry now? |
|---|---|---|
| Learning about the culture of Catholics in the United States | 69% | 44% |
| Learning about the culture of the United States generally | 65 | 42 |
| Parish administration and finances | 64 | 49 |
| U.S. pronunciation | 60 | 45 |
| Learning about the history and ecclesiology of the Catholic Church in the United States | 60 | 42 |
| Pastoral counseling | 56 | 48 |
| Ministry to engaged and married couples | 51 | 43 |
| Working with lay parish leaders | 49 | 39 |
| Dealing with prejudice | 48 | 36 |
| Social concerns ministry | 47 | 41 |
| Personal health and exercise | 45 | 39 |
| Preparing homilies and preaching | 44 | 37 |
| Youth ministry | 43 | 38 |
| Working with women | 43 | 32 |
| Computer technology and the Internet | 42 | 40 |
| Language study other than English | 36 | 39 |
| Working with permanent deacons | 31 | 29 |

Source: CARA's 2012 national survey of international priests

Finally, some respondents mentioned that the opportunity for ongoing formation and classes would be a welcome addition to acculturation programs like IPI. Said one, it would be helpful "to have ongoing programs or formation" or to "have one or two formators who are mobile to the site we are doing our ministry." Said another, the "IPI could conduct a second-time gathering with the same participants for at least one week to share and learn more with the experiences" they have had since the program ended. Another went even further, suggesting "that every year the IPI [cohorts] could come [back] for a week for sharing," adding that such sharing "would help us a lot."

This sentiment was echoed in the survey of international priests, as shown in Table 3.6. There are many areas of continuing formation that the priests report would be useful for them *currently*. For example, nearly half of respondents say that continuing formation on parish administration and finances and on pastoral counseling would be "very helpful" to their ministry now. About two in five say that continuing formation on the culture of Catholics in the United States, ministry to engaged and married couples, U.S. pronunciation, working with lay parish leaders, social concerns, and personal health and exercise would be "very helpful" to them now.

Respondents were also asked if they would recommend IPI to other incoming international priests. The responses were a resounding "yes"—the priests see the program as a good introduction to U.S. culture, parish life, and language. Said one, "It is a great experience to hear about the Church in the U.S." Another mentioned the importance of the program because "in the parishes, no one is going to teach us," asking: "How can we learn? Who is going to teach us?" The program, according to one respondent, "bettered my English (American)," while another said it helped him "function with courage and confidence."

## POTENTIAL REASONS FOR CHOOSING A PARTICULAR ACCULTURATION PROGRAM

When asked what factors would be important to them in choosing an acculturation program now, international priests responding to the national survey rated three practical considerations as being potentially most influential: convenience of the program dates (rated by 61 percent as "very much" an influence), the location (57 percent), and the length of the program (55 percent). However, for slightly more than half of respondents, positive feedback from other priests who have participated in the program and whether the program appears to be a good fit for priests of their particular nationality or culture are also rated as potentially "very" influential. This suggests that it is the international priests' networks that are vital to the success of these programs, even more so than cost. See Table 3.7 for more information.

**Table 3.7** *If you were choosing now among continuing formation or acculturation programs for international priests, how much would these factors influence your choice?*

(Percentage responding "very much")

| | |
|---|---|
| Convenience of the program dates | 61% |
| Convenience of the program location | 57 |
| Length of the program | 55 |
| Positive feedback from other priests who have participated in the program | 54 |
| Whether the program appears to be a good fit for priests of my particular nationality or culture | 52 |
| Cost | 43 |
| Aspects of the program not offered by other programs | 35 |
| Whether the program is usually used by priests of my diocese or community | 35 |
| An advertisement or brochure about the program | 25 |

Source: CARA's 2012 national survey of international priests

## CONCLUSION

Acculturation programs are necessary for international priests serving in the United States and are recommended by the U.S. Conference of Catholic Bishops. Some dioceses have their own acculturation program for their international priests, others send their men to one of a handful of acculturation programs that have been developed around the country, but most dioceses deal with the acculturation needs of their international priests only on an *ad hoc* basis. While less than half of international priests have participated in such a program, and while programs vary in terms of length, timing, and formality, the international priests who have participated in such programs find them to be beneficial. More attention to such programs can only help the international priest in his ministry.

In the next chapter, we explore the parish experience of international priests. We also hear from parishioners in parishes with international priests who have gone through an acculturation program.

# CHAPTER 4
## Parish Life and the International Priest—
## Two Perspectives

The majority of international priests (75 percent) are ministering in a parish setting, either as pastor of one or more parishes, parochial vicar, or some other parish-based ministry. Of great concern, then, is how these international priests are adapting to parish life in the United States. There are two perspectives to consider in this pastoral reality: those of the parishioners at such parishes and those of the international priests themselves. Are American parishioners open to having international priests serve at their parish? What are the challenges they face when an international priest is assigned to their parish? Are international priests prepared for such placement in American parishes? How do they cope with the linguistic and cultural challenges of a parish-based placement? As the number of international priests serving in parish ministry continues to rise, these questions become more and more pertinent to the inclusion of such priests in the Church landscape of the United States.

## PERSPECTIVE ONE: VIEWS FROM THE PEWS

One way to measure the awareness and acceptance of international priests into the life of the American parish is to ask American Catholics. In 2000[10]

---

[10] The 2000 CARA Catholic Poll was a telephone poll of more than 2,500 adult self-identified Catholics conducted in January and February 2000. We asked a subset of 1,720 the series of questions about ways of meeting parish ministry needs. Following standard assumptions of statistical inference, a sample size of 1,720 yields a margin of sampling error of ±2.4 percent. In other words, characteristics and opinions of the individuals in the poll can be assumed to be within 2.4 percentage points of those for all self-identified Catholics in the nation.

and 2008,[11] CARA conducted national polls of adult U.S. Catholics that asked about support or opposition to various approaches to meeting the ministry needs of parishes in a time of fewer priests. Catholics were asked about their awareness of the declining number of priests in the United States. About two in three American Catholics have noticed a declining number of priests in recent years, and of those who have noticed about one in seven (15 percent) has been personally affected (see Table 4.1).

| Table 4.1 *As you may know, the number of priests in the United States has declined in recent decades. Have you noticed this change? [If "yes"] Have you personally been affected by this change?* | | |
|---|---|---|
| | **2000** | **2008** |
| Have noticed the change | 66% | 66% |
| Noticed but have *not* been personally affected | 47 | 51 |
| Noticed and have been personally affected | 19 | 15 |
| Source: CARA Catholic Polls, 2000 and 2008 | | |

As a follow-up to this question, CARA asked respondents to think about some of the ways that parishes and dioceses have been coping with a decline in the number of Catholic priests and to indicate which of these alternatives is most attractive. The results of these polls suggest that American parishioners are more open to the inclusion of international priests at their parish than one might expect. Bringing in priests from another country was supported by more than half of respondents (56 percent) in 2008. It should be noted that this is a slight *decline* from the 2000 poll, where 69 percent of respondents supported bringing in priests from another country to cope with a decline

---

[11] In 2008, CARA conducted a poll for the Department of Communications of the United States Conference of Catholic Bishops (USCCB). The questions about parish ministry needs were repeated, in amended form, and asked of all respondents. The margin of sampling error for this poll is ±3.1 percent. This poll was conducted via the Internet through Knowledge Networks, a respected Web survey organization. Participants in its polls are drawn from a nationally representative panel of households that has been compiled through traditional random telephone sampling.

in priests. However, the wording of the questions shifted slightly from 2000 (where respondents were asked if they favor or oppose international priests generally) to 2008 (where respondents were asked if they favor or oppose international priests in their parish specifically). This decline, then, may be an effect of a wording change in the question, or it might be a genuine shift in acceptance of international priests.

Regardless whether the change is due to question wording or a genuine change in attitude, more than half of respondents in 2008 supported bringing in priests from another country to cope with the declining number of Catholic priests in the United States. Those respondents who are involved in parish ministries or activities are regular Mass attenders, and those who have noticed a decline in the number of priests and have been personally affected by it are the most likely to support bringing in a priest from outside of the United States to serve in parish ministry in a time of fewer priests.

Additional surveys of American Catholics support this willingness to have international priests as the head of American parishes. A survey conducted in 2011 and outlined in *American Catholics in Transition* (D'Antonio et al. 2013:39) demonstrates that Catholics are more willing to have an international priest as the head of a parish than to have a deacon or a lay person as the head, to close the parish, or even to reduce the number of Saturday evening and Sunday Masses. Only sharing a priest with another parish or merging two or more nearby parishes into one parish are more favorable than bringing in an international priest, and the differences are not statistically significant. See Figure 4.1 for these data.

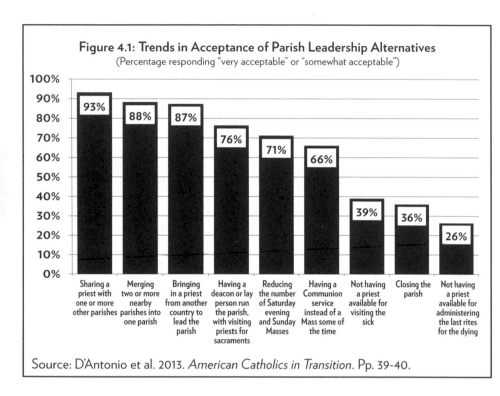

Figure 4.1: Trends in Acceptance of Parish Leadership Alternatives
(Percentage responding "very acceptable" or "somewhat acceptable")

Source: D'Antonio et al. 2013. *American Catholics in Transition.* Pp. 39-40.

These data suggest that a majority of Catholics support the inclusion of international priests in parishes in the United States. But survey data cannot provide the nuanced picture of what the ministry of these priests is really like. To understand more fully the perceptions of parishioners about the ministry of these priests, we conducted focus groups at three parishes in different parts of the country that were headed by priests from outside of the United States. We asked parishioners to tell us about their satisfaction and experiences with international priests, both currently and in the past, and their recommendations for preparation for international priests to serve in the United States.

## A Positive Addition

Generally, parishioners see the international priest as a positive for their community. For some, the parish would be without pastoral leadership or might be closed or otherwise merged without the international priest. One respondent mentioned that the parish has "been without a priest and [has] suffered that before" and that they have been "blessed with three or four international priests" in recent years. He went on to say that with the inclusion of the international priests at this very rural parish:

> We have been able to actually go here within our own town and not have to travel long distances to be able to go talk to a priest. You have someone that [serves as] a confidant in that spiritual way, and you have that ability to go [talk to him]. When you're in the community and you rely on that person to be there for you in your faith and it's taken away from you . . . and then you're *blessed* with these international priests, you know what it is to really have that and yearn for that.

Another participant from this same group mentioned that because of the parish's very rural location, "when there's a shortage of priests we're the first ones to lose . . . we lose out because we're small and if [the diocese doesn't] have [a priest] for you, they don't have one for you. There's been times when we haven't had a priest or had a different priest come in on the weekends and . . . it's a whole lot better" with the international priest.

## Cultural and Linguistic Challenges

Although the international priests are generally accepted, there are some challenges to their placement in American parishes, particularly with regard to cultural and linguistic differences. The most mentioned issue facing international priests upon their assignment to an American parish is language difficulties. For some, the priest's accent was difficult to understand. Said one, "I feel that when Father first came here I had some instant difficulty understanding some of the things he was saying, and it's only because of his accent." However, this participant went on to say that "now that I'm used to him, I just listen for certain inflections because he's doing inflections in some of his words differently than we do—I understand him very well now, but I did have some difficulty in the beginning." Asked whether this increased understanding is a product of the priest's increased linguistic abilities, the participant mentioned that it is both the priest learning to speak more standard English and the parishioners learning to understand the accent better. In this way, learning the language is a symbiotic process: not only do the priest's language abilities increase, but the parishioners' ability to understand what he is saying also increases with exposure to the accent.

A few focus-group participants shared stories of requests being "lost in translation," particularly in the early days of the international priest's ministry. These stories were usually amusing anecdotes of misspoken words, as illustrated below:

> I and another person were coordinating [the international priest's arrival at the parish], and we asked Father, "Do you need anything?" He said, "Yes." We said, "Okay." So he hands us a list, and it's something [I'll] never forget; he said, "two cushion, three cushion." I'm thinking, okay, he's from another country [and] maybe they like to sit down on cushions, so that's what he needs; so I asked what size and he says, "You know: two people, two cushions. Three people, three cushions." I looked at the [other parishioner] and said, "A couch and a loveseat!" So that was one of the things, you know . . .
>
> (Everyone laughs)
>
> And then we get to the store to buy groceries, and he kept on saying what sounded like celery to us. We took him to the vegetables, and it was not there. Finally, he tells us breakfast food—it was cereal—but yes, that was

one of the language barriers. You get through it, but
those are the little things you remember.

However, some respondents mentioned that the international priest will occasionally include his native language in celebrations and events. For the most part, the inclusion of this additional language is welcomed, as evidenced by this back-and-forth response at a parish in Baltimore, Maryland:

I notice that when we have special occasions, he likes
to insert the different languages into maybe a song
or a prayer, and, personally, I love it, because I'm into
language. I love to be able to see the English language,
and the very same thing in another language, and be
able to read it and know it's the same prayer. Quite
often, Father will break out into song in his native
language, and he'll lead us, and we'll eventually follow
and sing right along. It is quite rewarding, it's different,
but it's enjoyable.

(All agree)

Yes, it is quite enjoyable. I'm open to that kind of thing,
and I think other parishioners are, too.

[This experience helps us to] remind ourselves that
we are universal; Catholic means universal, and what
he brings to the table is that universality [that is] the
Church.

Two of the three international priests in these focus groups were multilingual. Participants mentioned that not only were these priests learning English, they have experience learning other languages—one, for example, is learning Spanish in addition to English to meet the needs of parishioners. Because of the multicultural nature of the parishes where some international priests are assigned, multiple language skills are seen as a priority. An exchange from a parish in southwest Texas outlines the need for, in this case, Spanish skills:

> I think it would be great if [international priests assigned to this parish] knew their Spanish when they started. In a parish like this, right here, we have a lot of Spanish people, and Father did not know Spanish when he started here. But he learned it. It sure would be a good idea if he had that before he got here.
>
> Spanish would be as important as English.
>
> Yes, I think so.
>
> I work for him on Tuesdays, and he told me, "Speak to me in Spanish." And then he said, "Stop it, I don't understand it."
>
> (All laugh)

When conducting these focus groups, the issue of cultural challenges was also raised by the participants, though it was not as urgent a topic as language. The most commonly mentioned cultural mismatches involved food; this is particularly true for community gatherings where the inclusion of food is seen as a means of welcoming. One participant mentioned inviting their international pastor to her house to welcome him to the community, but found cooking for him "challenging" because she was aware "that these are *not* the foods [he would] eat" in his home country. Another suggested that the parishioners go out to lunch with the priest, only under the condition of "no curry."

When asked about potentially more sensitive issues of cultural differences, the parishioners were frank: in general, they found the international priests to be a welcome addition culturally to the parish. There is a recognition that the devotional practices of international priests can be more traditional than their American counterparts (one participant called this being more "institutional"), but for the most part the inclusion of prayers and celebrations not commonly included in American parish life was celebrated by participants.

According to one, the "more institutional" spirituality is "very helpful to our spirituality, too." Another remarked that the international pastor at his parish is more biblically literate, saying that he "remembers everything about it" and "can quote it to the word," and that the inclusion of more Scripture has prompted him to "start reading [the Bible]." One respondent did mention that the more "institutional" approach of international priests can "have a tendency to cause some conflict," but when asked to provide a specific example of such a conflict, she was unable to name one, suggesting that this conflict may be more of a perception than a lived reality at that parish.

## Interaction with Parish Groups

Beyond language and culture, focus-group participants were specifically asked about international priests in parish ministry. How do they interact with the various groups in the parish, including the parish council, the youth group, and the parish school? Is there any conflict over the role of the laity generally, and women in particular, in parish ministry? Participants pointed out that in most parish settings their international priest was cooperative, inclusive, and an asset to parish life. These participants also mentioned that the international priests are collaborative, they reach out to the larger community, and they are integrated into the parish community.

Collaboration with lay leaders and other parishioners seemed to be key to the successful ministry of the international priest. Said one, his international pastor "believes in collaboration, working together, trying to do something unified, and building a community of faithful," and does not "just [say] 'I'm the priest, do it my way.'" Another mentioned that the collaborative approach of their international pastor makes them feel "more involved," and that he finds the priest willing to "compromise and make it right" by listening to parishioners. While some speculated that this open collaboration might be a product of "trying to please the parish," or due to the multiple ministry sites at which some international priests minister, others suggested that it might "just have something to do with international priests" themselves, because these parishioners have had repeated positive experiences with foreign-born clergy.

Not only are these priests seen as accessible to the parish community, they are often portrayed as being involved with the larger community, in both informal ways (such as being visible outside of the rectory) and formal ways (such as inviting collaboration with other religious and community groups in the area). Participants describe the priest as a "bridge builder" within the community, both through outreach to the community and through bringing community concerns to the parish. At a focus group in northwest Texas, the participants remarked on how accessible their pastor is, saying:

> When [Father] first got here, I saw him everywhere:
> I saw him here, I saw him at rodeos, I saw him
> at parades, I saw him at school, and I saw him at
> basketball games, football games. I mean, he was
> everywhere, and he just talked to everybody. I don't
> know how he does it. He speaks to everyone and
> makes a connection with them. . . . I don't know, but
> I'm sure that helps: being able to converse outside of
> the church with the community.

In Baltimore, participants noted that their international pastor is "deeply" involved in "the everyday activities of social, economic, legislation, government . . . whatever is going on for this community," and even brought together other Africans in the area for an interreligious cultural event.

## PERSPECTIVE TWO: VIEW FROM THE ALTAR

Another view of the ministry of international priests comes from the priests themselves. To understand the nuances of the international priests' perceptions of parish ministry, both qualitative data (through focus groups) and quantitative data (through a national survey) were collected from the priests. In many ways, the concerns of the priests echoed those of the lay men and women in their pews.

We surveyed international priests in the United States to learn more about the experience of these priests in their ministry. The priests were asked a series of questions about the challenges they face in ministry. About two in ten to three in ten international priests currently serving in parish ministry responded that difficulty reaching people today, workload, language, and cultural and theological differences are "somewhat" or "very much" problems in their ministry.[12] These themes were also mentioned by international priests in the five focus groups of international priests (and those in the diocese who work with or minister with international priests) that we conducted.

Three in ten international priests serving as pastors mentioned that the difficulty in reaching people today is "somewhat" or "very much" a problem in their current ministry. This topic—adjustments to U.S. culture—was also widely discussed in the focus groups of international priests across the country. Priests described differing ways of looking at the parish that are not necessarily the same here in the United States as in their native country.

## The Role of the Parish

In attempting to reach the Catholics in their area, some priests recognized that there was a mismatch between the role of the parish in their home diocese and the role of the parish in the American Catholic experience. As one Indian priest in a midwestern diocese described it:

> At one time, the parish was the center and focus of attention. It is no longer the center of attention as it might be in India. Here, people have gone other places. In Lent, we no longer have Stations of the Cross on Fridays because we only got ten people. We switched to Wednesdays and got fifty people. I don't know why, but

---

[12] The findings from this survey of international priests are discussed more fully in Chapter 5.

> I think it is because so many Catholics want to go out
> on a Friday. At one time, they would go to the Church
> because that is where the activity and the action was
> happening. It doesn't happen like that anymore. It is a
> cultural change more than anything else.

Another priest in the mid-Atlantic area mentioned that there is a different "pastoral method" that he used "when preaching to people in the United States" because here "we are losing people." He went on to ask: "How do you preach to people who are well-to-do and think they don't need God, and their family members are asking them why do you still go to church? That kind of ministry is very different!"

## Linguistic Challenges

The pastoral challenge of reaching American Catholics in the pews is exacerbated by the linguistic challenges facing the international priests. More than one in four international priests serving in a parish setting (27 percent) say that making themselves understood to others is "somewhat" or "very much" a problem in their current ministry setting. As was highlighted by those in the pews, the language barriers are more complicated than simply vocabulary and pronunciation; multilingual parishes need multilingual priests, and regional differences in language can also lead to misunderstandings or frustrations. In the case of one international priest in the mid-Atlantic region, a conversation with a woman in the parish took an unexpected turn due to language and cultural differences:

> An older lady gave [me] a ride to church, and after
> Mass [I] thanked the lady by saying "this wonderful
> older lady." She took immediate offense, but in [my]
> culture it is a term of endearment and respect.

Another international priest ministering in the Midwest mentioned a simple word, "y'all," being confusing, saying, "I had to make an effort to make changes in my speech to fit [y'all] in. That was a little thing; I can imagine it is a much bigger issue" for other words in other places.

Likewise, many international priests—especially those from India—have been speaking and studying English for many years. However, their understanding of the language does not necessarily take into account the cultural differences or the accent of their American pastoral placement. One Indian priest in the southern part of the Midwest explained that parishioners at his parish had confronted him about his language abilities, to which he exclaimed, "I have been speaking English for 20 years; how can you say that I'm not speaking right?" He went on to say:

> My experience in the parish is that one of the major problems in the culture is struggling with the parishioners. I get the idea that it is the collective American way—it is only right if it is done the way Americans do it. Pronunciation and language—we always try. We are always trying to do it the right way. I find it very difficult to pronounce some words; it is difficult. I could not pronounce Illinois. But, the way we are trying so hard, I see that the parishioners are asking them to do it our way. There isn't necessarily friction, but there is an expectation that we will learn the "correct way."

An African priest from the same diocese shared an experience from his seminary training where an American priest was teaching a class. He found that it "took [him] a long time to understand [the American priest] because of his accent. This led me to not understand him fully; it was difficult." This priest went on to say that international priests "should invite people to put themselves in our shoes and . . . have the same challenges we have here."

Even for those who have been speaking English for some time, the American cultural milieu around the language causes challenges. One priest in the mid-

Atlantic area described a situation where the custom of pleasantries in the United States caused some friction for an international priest, saying:

> People offer, "What can I do for you?" And the priest
> thinks, "Everyone wants to help me and my family!"
> And it can get out of hand. There was one priest where
> someone kept asking, "What can I do to help you?"
> After a few months, the priest came down with a
> laundry list of needs. The person complained that now
> the priest wants everything! Asking, "What are your
> needs? How can I help?" is just being polite.

Less prominent—but still present—was the conversation about the need for the international priests to be able to speak multiple languages. One priest highlighted that, in some cases, "foreign clergy work with people from where they are from," and that this kind of placement may mitigate some of the need for multilingualism. Another Polish priest assigned to a diocese on the West Coast described that "first [he] learned English. Then, [he] learned Spanish" in order to function more effectively at his assigned parish.

## The Role of the Priest

Related to the challenge of reaching American Catholics are the theological and cultural differences between the sending country and the United States on the role of the priest in the Church. In fact, one in five international priests currently assigned to parish ministry say that theological differences in the concept of the priesthood are "somewhat" or "very much" a challenge in his current ministry placement. In many cases, international priests described their role in their home country as being one of higher social status than in the United States and having to adjust to this difference once they were assigned to a parish in the United States.

One Indian priest in a diocese in the Plains region of the United States described the difference in the status of the priest between his home diocese and his assigned diocese as "stark," saying that, in India, the priest is "the father of the family," but in the United States, "there are concerns around money and law" that are not present in his home diocese. A Filipino priest in the Midwest described a difference in the role of the priest:

> There is a big difference. In the Philippines, the priest
> is on a pedestal. The bishop is even more. The Church
> was organized in the Philippines earlier than the
> government! The Church is so powerful. We have
> Christmas, and parties—the life of the people is run
> by the Church. In the Philippines, we don't have
> abortion or divorce. The idea here is that the respect
> of the priest is so high. In America, it is so different.
> The expectation is different. I was serving the Mexican
> community, and they respect the priests. But, to the
> Caucasians, the priest is just an ordinary guy in the
> Church.

Some participants mentioned that a major difference in the understanding of the priesthood between the sending country and the United States is rooted in the relative poverty of the sending country. A priest from Nigeria ministering on the West Coast mentioned that "poverty has a lot to do with the differences," because, "in many communities, the priest is the educated member of the community." A second Nigerian priest in this same focus group described the priesthood in Nigeria as "culturally spoiled," adding that "once you are ordained a priest, you become something in the lordship category" and that "people are supposed to take care of you." He found this to be a key difference from the place of the priest in the United States. This was echoed by an Indian priest, also ministering on the West Coast:

> If you grow up in a very poor country, there are so
> many poor people and people who are just surviving,
> it is spread throughout the culture. So that any family
> who is middle class will not be doing any manual
> labor. They will not take out the garbage, they will not

cook, they will not clean. So, if you go to seminary, you
are accustomed to being served. You've never had to
wash your own clothes or cook your own food. It is
really a major adjustment when they come here. The
reality for these people is that it is a major shift.

Others mentioned that the cultural differences in the understanding of the
role of the priest come from a better educated laity in the United States. One
international priest in the Midwest articulated this difference, saying that
priests "who come here from other . . . countries are not expecting to find
lay people as well versed as many Catholics are in this country." He went on
to exclaim, "It is amazing how many lay people have Ph.D.s in Scripture and
theology who are floating around our parishes; some places you have to be
careful what you say!"

A priest from India ministering in the Plains region said that the difference
lies in the "administration of the parish," noting that "in India . . . the Church
provides education, health, social [services], and more," but in the United States
"the people are self-sufficient, and the people provide to the Church." There
is a reversal in the role of the priest and the parish between the countries:
"In India, the people are depending on [the priests] and [the priests] provide
direct guidance," but in the United States, "the priest works in a collaborative
way with the people," and parish life is "more complicated."

It should be noted, however, that 10 percent or fewer of international priests
serving in parish ministry said that working with lay leaders, conflict with
parishioners or laity, and difficulty of working with women is "somewhat" or
"very much" a problem in their current ministry, suggesting that while these
differences are noted, they are not necessarily sources of serious problems in
the international priests' parish ministry.

# EASING THE TRANSITION

The international priest in parish ministry faces challenges—linguistically, culturally, and pastorally. These same challenges can be present for those in the pews as well. We asked parishioners and international priests what resources and tools would be most useful for easing the transition to an international priest. In some cases, the suggestions were similar from both sides of the altar; in other cases, specific suggestions were made for orienting and welcoming the international priest to parish ministry.

## Suggestions from the Priests

On the national survey of international priests described earlier, we asked the priests an open-ended question: "What resources would help you in your priestly ministry in the United States?" While the responses to this question ranged in topic, some of the priests mentioned resources related to pastoral ministry, particularly with regard to the administration of the parish, cultural challenges, and the need for welcoming and patience from parishioners.

Many international priests mentioned the need for more administrative support in their parish ministry. Some mentioned the need for staffing generally, including the need for "a good administrator," and "having the right personnel with which to work" as being "ideal." Others said they needed more lay leadership, saying that a resource that would be helpful would be to "prepare lay people for administration" of the parish. Still a third group mentioned the need for training in administrative duties, calling for "formation on leadership [and] management," and asking for "training on how to use a secretary and how to be organized."

During the regional focus groups, several priests mentioned that Catholic parishes in the United States are in some ways more complex than parishes in other countries. One participant noted that "even a small parish here is a big parish in India," while another pointed out that it is the parish "committees" that can be a source of frustration, adding that his "advice would be to any priest to be respectful and sit down with a committee and figure out what we are going to do together as a team."

International priests also recognize the need for additional cultural training to prepare them for ministry in an American parish. These responses included the need for language training—especially accent reduction and Spanish-language skills—as well as general cultural training. Some requested more information on the history of the United States. Said one, a resource that would help in his priestly ministry would be "to learn the history [of] the USA," while another mentioned that he "always felt that something was missing, that it was not enough just to learn the language," adding that additional training "about the culture and reality of the people and the church" would be a resource that would help him in his priestly ministry.

A few mentioned that training on different cultural groups within their ministry setting would be helpful. Said one, a resource would be "continuing education [on the] dialogue of cultures," while another mentioned a need for "a brochure that briefly describes the main cultural differences [between] the American and Hispanic cultures." One priest in Los Angeles echoed this tightrope walk between cultures, saying:

> Find a priest that would function in a parish as if there
> was only one parish. The reality is that there are two
> parishes: the Hispanic parish and the English-speaking
> parish. . . . It is very hard to get the whole parish
> together for a common program. They prefer everyone
> to be on their own: one in English and one in Spanish.
> We have a few multicultural Masses, but the rest are all
> English or Spanish, even Holy Saturday. All the feasts
> are English and Spanish. In that case, you could have a
> priest who cannot function in one sector of the parish
> but could function in another. . . . At the same time, it
> is frustrating to have two parishes under one roof. If
> you try to do bilingual, they are more frustrated. If you

do English, they are happy; if you do Spanish, they are
happy.

Finally, some priests mentioned the need for parishioners to be patient and welcoming to the international priest. Said one, a resource for his ministry would be "having people who are open-minded and ready to share their thoughts" with him. Another mentioned the need for "more contact with people at any time, not just Sunday Mass," while a third called for "the support of the people." Likewise, a participant in a regional gathering in Washington, D.C., who works for a diocese preparing parishes to receive international priests, also recommended patience and preparation:

> International priests come from different parts of
> the world. Whenever any priest is coming from the
> outside, I explain to the people ahead of time that this
> priest is coming. Before an international priest comes,
> it is good to groom the people. Let them know. Let
> them talk about it. Let them know that this person
> coming in has his own cultural beliefs; it will take him
> time to function as an American. People need patience.
> Let them know that even if he makes a mistake, we
> need to have patience. It takes time.

## Suggestions from the Parishioners

Parishioners also had suggestions for easing the transition of international priests to parish ministry in the United States. These suggestions generally centered on three themes: topical training for the priest, preparation training for the parishioners, and a general attitude of acceptance and patience by both parties to ease the transition.

Parishioners most frequently brought up topical training as a primary way to help international priests ease their transition to ministry in the United States. The topics most mentioned were language and communication skills. Others noted that the administration of American parishes is complex, echoing the priests' sentiments. One mentioned that the bishops should be "very careful about where they place" international priests because "being able to do everything [including] finances . . . would probably overwhelm a new [international] priest."

Others mentioned steps that parishioners can take to help ease the transition for an international priest into an American parish. These suggestions ranged from patience and understanding to a deep appreciation for the presence of a resident priest. One focus group participant in Baltimore, Maryland, summed it this way:

> I would say do your homework. Be prepared, whatever you're given. Make sure you get it early because we tried to do some nice things here to show him that we knew where he had come from. We had someone bake a beautiful cake and signify his home. We went out and got maps and flags, and we really wanted to let him know that we didn't know everything about his country and all that went on there, but we were welcoming. I think that's a great beginning for anyone, you know.

> So that's the lesson perhaps; to welcome.

> Absolutely.

> Be patient.

> And be understanding on both ends. This person is coming a long way from his home. He leaves his home and his family because we need his help over here.

Finally, several participants noted that parishioners receiving an international priest must have an attitude that is welcoming and patient. Said one: "Love, respect, and cooperation. I think that goes a long way . . . whether they're Spanish, Irish, coming from Nigeria . . . if you don't have those three, then what will you have?" Another, from the same focus group in southwestern Texas, mentioned "revelation, relationship, and communication," saying that these three elements are "what you base any relationship on. Any relationship you come across, you have to have communication; revelation is getting to know each other; and then hanging around and doing the work to have the relationship." In another focus group in Texas, a participant mentioned the need to be "open-minded, open-hearted, and open to the adaptation to different cultures."

# CONCLUSION

In their ministry in parish life, international priests struggle with a cultural mismatch between the expectations and role of the priest and the parish in American Catholics' lives, as well as linguistic challenges, including the need for proficiency in multiple languages. To ease the transition to American parish life, international priests suggest additional language and cultural training for themselves, and cultural training and an attitude of welcoming and acceptance for their parishioners.

Similarly, those parishioners in parishes with international priests report cultural and linguistic issues—including understanding incoming priests' accents—as well as interactions with parish groups as being possible sources of conflict for the ministry of the international priest, though most parishioners report being very happy with the ministry of the international priest at their parish.

In the next chapter we explore the satisfactions and challenges of ministry for international priests serving in the United States. We make some comparisons between U.S.-born and international priests in their evaluations of their ministry.

# CHAPTER 5
## Satisfaction with Ministry and Challenges in Ministry

The greatest joy has been serving God's people in the teaching office of priesthood and the sanctified office when I celebrate the sacraments. In my first years of priesthood I even confirmed two people at the Easter Vigil. Celebrating the sacraments and teaching God's words have been the greatest joy during these years of priesthood.

—An international priest from Mexico

Priests who choose to leave their home country for a new life and ministry in another demonstrate a particularly high level of self-sacrifice and commitment—standing apart among a group of men who are already highly dedicated by virtue of their vocation. International priests in the United States clearly care deeply about service to the Church and serving the people of God. This is the mark of someone who is likely to find many great joys in life.

Being an international priest, however, may sometimes bring its own special difficulties. Leaving behind family and friends to begin a new life in a foreign country may exacerbate the feelings of loneliness that some priests experience—especially if they have difficulty forming friendships with the priests of their new diocese. Having to adapt to a new culture—and possibly win over parishioners hesitant about being served by a priest who does not share that culture—may add to the many challenges of daily ministry. In this chapter, we draw on responses to the 2012 national survey to examine both happiness and problems in the lives and ministry of international priests.

## Happiness with Priestly Life and Ministry

Respondents were asked how happy they are with several aspects of their lives and ministry. Table 5.1 shows the responses. The first of these is particularly important because it is a "summary" item that reflects their overall happiness in their life as a priest. Nearly nine in ten international priests, 88 percent, describe themselves as "very" happy.

| Table 5.1 Happiness with Various Aspects of Priestly Life and Ministry | | | |
|---|---|---|---|
| | "Very" Happy | "Somewhat" Happy | "Not at All" or "Only a Little" Happy |
| Your life as a priest | 88% | 9% | 3% |
| Your sacramental and liturgical ministry | 81 | 17 | 2 |
| Your relationship with your bishop or religious superior | 71 | 20 | 9 |
| Your present living situation | 68 | 27 | 5 |
| Your personal spiritual life | 68 | 27 | 5 |
| Conditions for ministry in your diocese | 55 | 35 | 10 |
| Your relationship with U.S.-born priests | 51 | 39 | 10 |
| Your present financial situation | 49 | 42 | 9 |
| Practices of governance in your diocese or religious institute | 49 | 36 | 15 |
| The retirement plan offered by your diocese | 44 | 30 | 26 |

Note: Rows may not total 100 due to rounding.
Source: CARA's 2012 national survey of international priests

Levels of happiness in being a priest are highest for international priests in ministry in the Midwest, with 92 percent saying they are "very" happy, and only slightly lower for those in the Northeast, with 86 percent expressing this level of happiness. Thus generalized happiness is expressed regardless of where international priests are assigned in the United States.

There is also little variation in happiness related to when international priests were ordained. Those who were priests for many years before coming to the United States, having been ordained at least ten years prior to entering, express the most happiness, with 91 percent saying they are "very" happy in their life as a priest. By comparison, 87 percent of those who were ordained within a decade of coming to the United States express this level of happiness. There is slight variation by age upon entry to the United States. Priests who came to the United States at the age of forty or older are the most likely to say they are "very" happy in their life as a priest (91 percent). Eighty-two percent of those who entered the country before the age of thirty responded similarly in the survey.

Where international priests are immigrating from also has an impact. About seven in ten international priests (73 percent) from an English-speaking country (i.e., Ireland, the United Kingdom, or Canada) as well as those from other areas of Europe (68 percent) say they are "very" happy in their life as a priest. More express this level of happiness who are coming from Asia or the Pacific Islands (94 percent), Africa (92 percent), and Latin America (88 percent).

Synthesizing these results, international priests from developing countries who have been serving as priests for an extended period of time in their country of origin, who come to the United States in their forties or later to serve in a midwestern parish, are perhaps *most* likely to express the highest levels of happiness in being a priest in the United States. Yet, it is important to note that even those who come by some other set of circumstances and are in ministry elsewhere in the United States are still very likely to express happiness in their priestly life.

While most priests are "very" happy generally, there are some specific aspects of priestly life that they are not as likely to be this happy about. A slim majority, 51 percent, say they are "very" happy in their relationships with U.S.-born priests. There are variations in response to this question according to the international priests' countries of origin. About seven in ten of those from

English-speaking countries (71 percent) say they are "very" happy in their relationships with U.S.-born priests. Half of those from an Asian or Pacific Island country also express this level of happiness (50 percent). Minorities of international priests from elsewhere say they are "very" happy about this aspect, including 49 percent of those from an African country, 46 percent of those from Latin American countries, and 37 percent of those from a European country outside of the United Kingdom or Ireland. There is also regional variation based on where international priests come to minister in the United States. Just 46 percent of those in ministry in the American South say they are "very" happy with their relationship with U.S.-born priests compared with majorities serving elsewhere.

Aspects of priestly life that international priests express the most happiness include their sacramental and liturgical ministry (81 percent are "very" happy with this), their relationship with their bishop or religious superior (71 percent), their present living situation (68 percent), and their personal spiritual life (68 percent).

More than half of international priests, 55 percent, say they are "very" happy with the conditions for ministry in their diocese. Although region does not strongly affect general happiness, it does impact how satisfied international priests are about the conditions of ministry in their diocese. Only 40 percent of those in the Northeast say they are "very" happy with the conditions for ministry in their diocese, compared with 70 percent in the Midwest and 61 percent in the West. Forty-nine percent of those in the South say they are "very" happy with this aspect.

Other aspects of priestly life that international priests are not as likely to say they are "very" happy about include: their present financial situation (49 percent), the practices of governance in their diocese or religious institute (49 percent), and the retirement plan offered to them (44 percent). International priests who entered the United States at a younger age are more likely to be happy with their finances. Sixty-four percent of those entering the U.S. before the age of thirty say they are "very" happy with their financial situation, compared with 51 percent entering the United States in their thirties, and only 42 percent entering the country at age forty or older. Country of origin also appears to matter. Thirty-three percent of international priests from Latin America say they are "very" happy with their financial situation, compared with 54 percent of those who came from the English-speaking countries of Ireland, the United Kingdom, or Canada. This difference may in part reflect the level of financial well-being the priest had upon entering the United States.

Looking just at international priests who are "very" happy generally in their life as a priest (88 percent of the sample), many also indicate they are "very" happy with their sacramental and liturgical ministry (88 percent), their relationship with their bishop or religious superior (77 percent), their present living situation (75 percent), and their spiritual life (75 percent). Fewer say they are "very" happy with any other aspects. These elements of priestly life are likely at the "core" of what makes international priests happy overall.

International priests express a high degree of life satisfaction, similar to other U.S. priests generally, who are among the most highly satisfied group of people in our society. Table 5.2 shows this comparison. In a 2009 CARA study of priests from across the nation, U.S.-born and foreign-born priests expressed similar levels of happiness for most of the aspects about which they were asked.[13]

---

[13] The percentages from that survey are not perfectly comparable with percentages from this one due to slightly different wording in the response categories. The 2009 study was sponsored by the National Federation of Priests' Councils, and results are available in much greater detail in Gautier, Perl, and Fichter (2012).

### Table 5.2
### Selected Happiness with Aspects of Ministry: International and U.S.-Born Priests
(Percentage saying they are either "somewhat" or "very" happy with each)

|  | International | U.S.-born |
|---|---|---|
| Your sacramental and liturgical ministry | 98% | 98% |
| Your life as a priest | 97 | 97 |
| Your present living situation | 95 | 92 |
| Your personal spiritual life | 95 | 89 |
| Your present financial situation | 92 | 86 |
| Your relationship with your bishop or religious superior | 91 | 77 |
| Conditions for ministry in your diocese | 90 | 87 |
| Your relationship with U.S.-born priests | 90 | 91 |
| Practices of governance in your diocese or religious institute | 85 | 69 |

Note: Figures for U.S.-born priests come from the 2009 CARA survey for the National Federation of Priests' Councils. Wording of the NFPC response categories was "very happy" or "pretty happy." The NFPC survey asks about "your relationship with your brother priests" rather than with "U.S.-born priests."
Sources: International priests: CARA's 2012 national survey of international priests
U.S.-born priests: 2009 CARA survey for the National Federation of Priests' Councils

International priests were more likely than U.S.-born priests to say they were "somewhat" or "very" happy with their relationship with their bishop or religious superior (91 percent compared with 77 percent) and with the practices of governance in their diocese or religious institute (85 percent compared with 69 percent).

The 2012 survey of international priests included a total of ten items upon which happiness was gauged. To further explore these, a "Happiness Index" was created from these data. Respondents received a score of 1 for each item they indicated that they were at least "somewhat" happy with. Thus those who are the most happy could have a score of 10 on the index and those least happy could have a score of 0.

The average score for respondents was 8.8. A majority, 52 percent, score a 10 on the index. More than one in five (22 percent) score a 9. Only 6 percent of respondents have a score of less than 5, representing more dissatisfaction than happiness.

As shown in Figure 5.1, international priests from the Philippines, Mexico, Ghana, India, the United Kingdom, and Canada express the broadest levels of happiness with average scores of 9.0 or more. Clergy from Poland have a happiness index score of 8.7. Priests from Ireland and elsewhere in Europe are a bit less likely, on average, to be as happy, with average scores of 8.1 or lower.

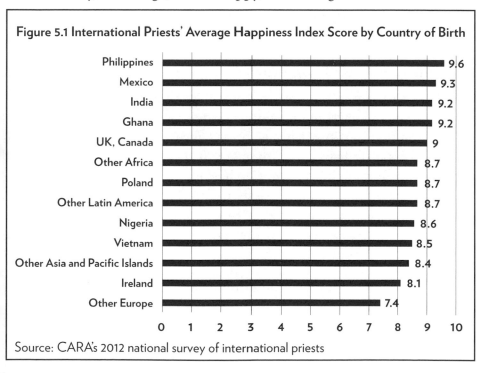

Figure 5.1 International Priests' Average Happiness Index Score by Country of Birth

Source: CARA's 2012 national survey of international priests

International priests expressing the highest levels of happiness, as measured by this index, include those who:

- Were born in the 1950s (9.3)

- Minister in English only (9.1)

- Are in dioceses with 100,000 to 399,999 Catholics (9.1)

- Participated in an orientation or acculturation program (9.0)

- Entered the United States in their thirties (9.0)

- Are in ministry in the West (9.0)

There are no significant differences in happiness between diocesan and religious international priests.

## Happiness in Their Own Words

Generally, people in service professions—for example, teachers, psychologists, and physical therapists—tend to be among the most satisfied in our society (University of Chicago News Office, 2007). Giving of oneself for others makes people happy. And this can only be strengthened in the context of a religious vocation in which one's whole life is structured around service. The survey asked international priests to describe, in their own words, the greatest joys they experience in their priestly ministry in the United States. As we see in their responses, below, they explicitly emphasize the centrality of service in priestly ministry:

> My greatest joy is the opportunity to serve God's people in my faith community. My faith community appreciates my dedication to priestly ministry, including celebrating the sacraments and visiting nursing homes, hospitals, and the homebound.

That my little service is not only greatly appreciated
by many but also requested; celebrating Mass, spiritual
direction.

Being able to serve people in need.

Serving people, especially in rural areas of the diocese,
offers great consolation and fulfillment as I watch
them grow in Catholic spirituality.

Serving the faithful through the celebration of the
sacraments and providing spiritual direction for my
parishioners. In addition, I enjoy sharing my faith with
the students I teach at the university.

More broadly, priestly ministry, especially parish ministry, situates one
in a web of relationships—within a community of people who care for one
another and who share a common zeal for living out their faith. Below,
international priests talk about the joys of community and their interactions
with parishioners. Some talk about how they not only give to their parishioners
but receive in return.

The people are receptive and respectful to priests. They
are concerned. Sometimes the priests have to make an
effort to meet them to talk. . . . I enjoy celebrating the
Eucharist for them. They appreciate and love it. They
express it, saying, "We are being cared for." That's joyful.

People are very appreciative and generous in their
compliments. I was appreciated not because of my role
as a priest, but because of my performance.

My relationship with my parishioners. They accept and
love me unconditionally.

The people I have come to know and love, especially at the current parish I am serving. They have become my family.

It is gratifying to work in a new environment where I am accepted fully by the people. A Catholic priest is accepted anywhere in the world. That is the universality of the Catholic Church. It is my greatest joy.

Other representative responses evoking a diversity of reasons for happiness among international priests include:

When people go beyond the discrimination and accept me as their priest, and invite me to their house there is no limit for my joy and happiness. I am available to them any time. So that makes me happy, because people are happy.

Happy to see people beaming with smiles, in spite of their sufferings and pain.

Being able to minister to people wherever I am needed. As a missionary, I am fulfilled that I am able to give to the Church as a missionary of St. Paul, as other missionaries gave to my people in Nigeria.

I can develop my talents to the full without being stifled by superiors, unlike in my own native country, where I have to ask permission for almost everything that I wanted to do. Here, I am responsibly accountable for my decisions; in my native country, I am always stifled.

I am so happy to see people who are coming back to the Church.

That I was able to help the faithful here in the United States, that I can be able to spread more my wings. And to see the life in the "bigger Church."

## Problems in Ministry

International priests were also asked about a variety of problems they face in their ministry. Many priests did not cite any of the items listed in the survey as being "somewhat" or "very much" a problem for them. As shown in Table 5.3, a quarter or more of international priests said the following were at least "somewhat" a problem: a shortage of available priests (36 percent), distance from home and family (36 percent), difficulty really reaching people (29 percent), adapting to cultural differences (29 percent), making oneself understood to others (26 percent), and the loneliness of priestly life (25 percent). These represent a mixture of issues related to being from another country and away from one's family and peers to core challenges in one's ministry as a priest.

### Table 5.3 *How much are these a problem to you in your ministry?*

(Percentage saying each is either "somewhat" or "very much" a problem)

| | |
|---|---|
| Shortage of available priests | 36% |
| Distance from home and family | 36 |
| Difficulty of really reaching people today | 29 |
| Adapting to cultural differences in the United States | 29 |
| Making myself understood to others | 26 |
| Loneliness of priestly life | 25 |
| Too much work | 24 |
| Theological differences in the concept of the priesthood | 24 |
| Unrealistic demands and expectations of lay people | 23 |
| Working with people from other cultures | 20 |
| Negative attitudes from laity you serve | 19 |
| Difficulty of working with U.S. priests | 17 |
| Immigration status and/or related paperwork | 16 |
| Relevance of the work I am assigned to do | 14 |
| Lack of opportunity for personal fulfillment | 14 |
| Being expected to represent Church teachings I have difficulty with | 13 |
| Pastoring more than one parish | 12 |
| Celibacy | 12 |
| Relationship with the bishop of the diocese where I currently minister | 11 |
| Working with lay leaders | 9 |
| Relationship with the bishop of my home diocese | 8 |
| Conflict with parishioners or laity | 7 |
| Difficulty of working with women | 5 |

Source: CARA's 2012 national survey of international priests

Only about one in ten or fewer cite the following as being at least "somewhat" a problem: their relationship with their bishop in their current diocese of their bishop at home (11 percent and 8 percent, respectively), working with lay leaders (9 percent), conflict with parishioners or laity (7 percent), or difficulty working with women (5 percent).

Although 49 percent of international priests did *not* indicate that they were "very" happy in their relationships with U.S.-born priests, only 17 percent say that difficulties working with U.S. priests is "somewhat" or "very" much a problem in their ministry. Few also cite their relationships with the laity as a problem for them. Only 23 percent cite unrealistic demands and expectations of lay people, and 19 percent indicate negative attitudes from laity they serve as at least "somewhat" a problem.

Overall, 24 percent of international priests cite theological differences in the concept of the priesthood as being at least "somewhat" a problem for them. This is most often the case for those in the Pre-Vatican II ordination class (those ordained prior to 1964). Forty-six percent of this subgroup cites theological differences as "somewhat" or "very much" a problem in their ministry, compared with less than three in ten of those in any later ordination cohorts. In general, international priests of this oldest ordination cohort are more likely than those ordained in more recent years to cite the following as being at least "somewhat" a problem: adapting to cultural differences (47 percent), their relationship with their bishop from their home diocese (42 percent), and the loneliness of priestly life (46 percent).

Four in ten international priests from Latin America (39 percent) cite theological differences as being at least "somewhat" a problem. Fewer from all other regions indicate this. Those from Latin America are also the most likely to cite making themselves understood to others (43 percent) and the relevance of the work they are assigned (26 percent) as being similarly important problems.

Overall, 13 percent of international priests indicate that having to represent Catholic Church teachings they have difficulty with is "somewhat" or "very much" a problem in their ministry. The likelihood of responding as such is related to how long they were ordained before coming to the United States. Only 7 percent of those ordained ten or more years before coming to the United States cite Church teachings as a problem. By comparison, 18 percent of those ordained less than ten years before coming to the United States indicate Church teachings being a problem. International priests from English-speaking countries (Ireland, the United Kingdom, and Canada) are by far the most likely to cite Church teachings as being problematic (38 percent).

As shown in Figure 5.2, international priests from Mexico, Vietnam, Poland, Ireland, and Asian and Pacific Island countries (excluding the Philippines and India) are the most likely to indicate that distance from their family or home is "somewhat" or "very much" a problem for them. Less than a quarter of international priests from Ghana, the United Kingdom or Canada, or other Latin American countries say this is at least "somewhat" a problem for them. There appears to be little or no relationship between the actual distance from these countries to the United States and the response patterns of international priests. For example, of all the countries listed, Mexico may be among the more readily accessible, but half of priests from this country cite distance from their family and home as a problem. By comparison, those from Ghana, much farther away from their home, are even less likely to say this is a problem for them (24 percent).

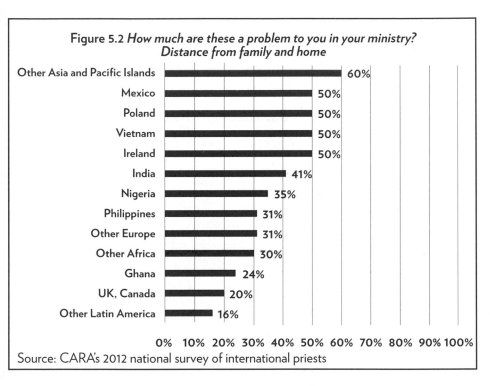

Figure 5.2 *How much are these a problem to you in your ministry?*
*Distance from family and home*

Source: CARA's 2012 national survey of international priests

The survey of international priests included a total of twenty-three items that respondents could identify as a problem. To further explore these, a "Problems Index" was created from these data, similar to the "Happiness Index." Respondents received a score of 1 for each item they indicated as being "somewhat" or "very much" a problem for them. These were then totaled and divided by twenty-three to convert the index to a 10-point scale consistent with the "Happiness Index." Thus those who say they face the most problems could have a score of 10 on the index and those facing the fewest problems could have a score of 0.[14]

The average score for respondents was 1.8. Forty-eight percent of respondents have a score of 1 or less on the index. Only 4 percent have a score of 7 or higher—including 1 percent scoring 10. As shown in Figure

---

[14] Respondents who did not answer any of the items, four individuals, were excluded.

5.3, international priests from Vietnam and other Asian and Pacific Island countries (excluding the Philippines) say they face more problems in their ministry than other international priests. Priests from Ireland, Mexico, the Philippines, and Poland also say they face more problems than the average international priest.

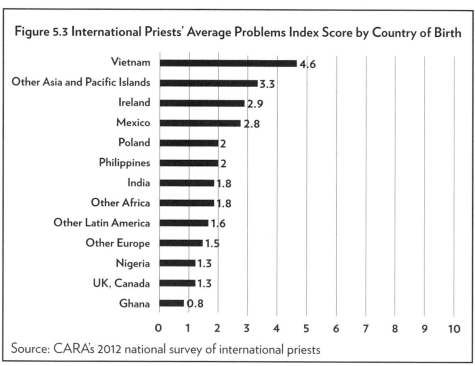

Figure 5.3 International Priests' Average Problems Index Score by Country of Birth

Source: CARA's 2012 national survey of international priests

The following subgroups of international priests have among the highest "Problems Index" scores, meaning they indicated multiple aspects of their ministry as problems for them:

- Those who entered the United States in their twenties (2.8)

- Those in dioceses with fewer than 100,000 Catholics (2.4)

- Those of the Pre-Vatican II ordination class (2.3)

- Those in ministry in the South (2.2)

- Those ordained less than ten years from entering the United States (2.1)

- Religious priests (2.0)

## Problems in Their Own Words

Below are some responses from the survey that were provided by international priests when they were asked to describe, in their own words, the "greatest challenge" they face in their priestly ministry in the United States. Responses tended to mirror the results from the closed-ended questions in the survey.

Some international priests cite issues related to the acceptance and welcome, or lack thereof, they feel from their fellow priests and their parishioners. These challenges are often cultural and linguistic. Prejudice is often mentioned as well.

> The readiness for some to remind you directly or indirectly that after all you are a foreigner, with these questions: Are you not missing home? When did you see your people last? When are you leaving? If you visit home this time, are you coming back?

> Discrimination and racial prejudice.

> Sometimes being seen as [an] "outsider."

> Being misunderstood sometimes and being misrepresented. My language accent, which some people still find not well reduced, especially when they are impatient or pretending not to hear or understand simply because I did not say it exactly the way they think it should be said.

> Lack of acceptance by some American-born priests, as well as lack of trust from them.

> Seminarians born outside the USA have so many challenges not only in pastoral work and the switch between their country-of-origin model of parish, and pastoral work and the model here, but also in their own psychological health trying to cope and adapt quickly with the levels of stress and life here in the USA.

> People trying to look down on you because of your accent and sometimes color.

> The state [where] I live now is very narrow-minded and prejudiced. I feel like they are just following the crowd. Just lip service. So individualistic, and they think there is no world outside of here.

Some priests mention the loneliness they feel as a priest as well as feelings of homesickness and a desire to see their family and friends.

> Being far away from family and friends back home.

> Cooking my food and sometimes eating alone.

> Not having other priests from my country around, especially my seminary colleagues.

> Living alone in the rectory was a challenging adjustment.

> Sometimes I feel a little bit lonely.

Some also note the demands put upon them in dioceses with few priests and the feeling that they are being treated as "supply" or "servant" priests.

The tendency to treat priests as "supply" or a sort of "priests for rent" thing.

As I grow older the pastoral responsibilities increase due to the shortage of priests.

Being a "servant" priest.

The small number of other priests who can speak Spanish.

Shortage of priests. Spread very thin.

Unrealistic expectations of some people and accentuated with the shortage of priests; heavy workload; fatigue and stress; the fear of burnout.

Too many demands and spiritual needs from the people, and we are just a few priests serving them. And too much pressure in the administrative things.

As shown in Table 5.4, in expressing the seriousness of problems facing them in their ministry, international priests are not all that similar to U.S.-born priests, who are generally more likely to identify the issues listed as at least "somewhat" problematic to them.[15] However, in relative terms, both samples of priests rank in similar order the issues that they consider problematic. Both U.S.-born and international priests cite a shortage of priests as being most problematic. Many in both samples also cite too much work, which may be a result of the priest shortage, and similarly both find their capacity to really reach people today challenging.

---

[15] The percentages from that survey are not perfectly comparable to percentages from this one due to slightly different wording in the response categories. The 2009 study was sponsored by the National Federation of Priests' Councils, and results are available in much greater detail in Gautier, Perl, and Fichter (2012).

Table 5.4
Selected Problems in Ministry: International and U.S.-born Priests
(Percentage saying each is either "somewhat" or "very much" a problem)

| | International | U.S.-born |
|---|---|---|
| Shortage of available priests | 36% | 68% |
| Difficulty of really reaching people today | 29 | 60 |
| Loneliness of priestly life | 25 | 40 |
| Too much work | 24 | 53 |
| Theological differences in the concept of the priesthood | 24 | 44 |
| Unrealistic demands and expectations of lay people | 23 | 54 |
| Lack of opportunity for personal fulfillment | 14 | 16 |
| Being expected to represent Church teachings I have difficulty with | 13 | 43 |
| Pastoring more than one parish | 12 | 22 |
| Celibacy | 12 | 35 |
| Relationship with the bishop of the diocese where I currently minister | 11 | 35 |
| Conflict with parishioners or laity | 7 | 28 |
| Difficulty of working with women | 5 | 4 |

Note: Figures for U.S.-born priests come from the 2009 CARA survey for the National Federation of Priests' Councils. Wording of the NFPC response categories was "a great problem" or "somewhat a problem."
Sources: International priests: CARA's 2012 national survey of international priests
U.S.-born priests: 2009 CARA survey for the National Federation of Priests' Councils

International priests are not as likely as U.S.-born priests to say that unrealistic demands and expectations of lay people are "somewhat" or "very much" a problem for them (23 percent compared with 54 percent). Similarly, international priests are much less likely to say that being expected to represent Church teachings they have difficulty with is at least "somewhat" problematic for them (13 percent compared with 43 percent).

# CONCLUSION

International priests overwhelmingly express happiness in their ministry in the United States. This is generally consistent with U.S.-born priests, and satisfaction among international priests is even more evident in comparing their assessments of the problems they face with U.S.-born priests. In a final analysis, subtracting each international priest's "Problems Index Score" from his "Happiness Index Score" a composite "Net Happiness Score" is calculated. The average score for this composite index is 7.1 out of a possible 10. Overall, 78 percent of international priests have a score of 5.0 or higher. Sixteen percent have a score above 0 but less than 5. Just 3 percent are in negative territory where they emphasize problems in their ministry more than happiness. It might be hard to find another group of Americans that expresses this much happiness and satisfaction with their work.

In the next chapter, we draw some conclusions and implications from the data we have collected here. We illustrate those recommendations with quotes from the regional reflection gatherings of international priests, bishops, and others who work with international priests in diocesan pastoral ministry.

# CHAPTER 6
## Lessons and Implications from the Research

My greatest challenge is not being seen and accepted
as a missionary priest, but being called an international
priest. When priests from America, Ireland, France,
Australia, and other countries came to Nigeria, we
received them, not as international priests, but as
missionary priests sharing in the priesthood of Jesus
Christ, with a message of salvation from Jesus. But
here in the United States, I am not seen and received
as a missionary who is here on request, but seen as an
international priest.

—Survey respondent from Nigeria

The international priests who are living and working in parishes in the United
States have a great deal to share about their experience. Their expectations for
ministry and their perspectives about ministry in the United States are often
quite different from the anecdotes shared by other priests and parishioners
who come in contact with them, as illustrated by the quote above.

To learn more from international priests about their adjustment to ministry
in the United States and about ways to facilitate a smoother transition across
cultures, CARA conducted five regional listening sessions in 2012 with
international priests and those who work with them. The listening sessions
included approximately twelve to fifteen international priests and other
diocesan personnel (including vicars for clergy, directors of continuing
education for clergy, chancellors, and others) and took place at San Angelo,
Texas; Belleville, Illinois; Oklahoma City, Oklahoma; Los Angeles, California;
and Washington, D.C.

Representatives at each of the dioceses arranged the groups, and the meetings were held at a convenient location, such as a chancery conference room or a retreat center. The primary purpose of these gatherings was to learn from the international priests and those who work with them more about the experiences and needs of international priests. The sessions also provided an opportunity to present the CARA research on international priests serving in the United States that has been laid out in this book. That research was the basis for our listening sessions.

Each regional gathering began with an introductory presentation on the background of the project and the history of international priests in the United States, followed by a summary of key findings from CARA's research on international priests. The priests and others assembled at the regional gatherings were then asked to reflect on the presentations in light of their own experiences in ministry. The pages that follow here present a summary of the principal themes that emerged from these group discussions. We quote extensively from the priests themselves because, although each priest is unique, their collective experience reinforces the results of the research and illustrates the important points in a way that numbers cannot. We end each section with some of our own reflections and insights from others about the possible implications of this research for the Church in the United States and the international priests that serve here.

## ADVANCE PREPARATION FOR PRIEST AND PARISHIONERS

This seems obvious, but one of the most basic lessons drawn from the experiences of the international priests is that priests cannot and should not be treated as interchangeable parts. These international priests are usually very well prepared to celebrate the Mass and other sacraments. They do not arrive, however, with knowledge that is specific to U.S. cultural norms nor to the U.S. diocese in which they will work, such as the diocesan requirements for couples preparing for marriage or how the diocese handles the canonical process for people seeking an annulment. Many international priests have little or no experience in working with a parish pastoral council or collaborating in ministry with lay women.

For some, even basic life skills such as driving a car or cooking a meal may seem foreign at first. And though the priest may be comfortable celebrating Mass in English, parishioners may still have a difficult time adjusting to his accent, his mannerisms, his leadership style, and so forth. A little advance preparation, for both the international priest and the parishioners that will receive him, can go a long way in smoothing the transition for all involved.

Every diocese that accepts an international priest follows its own process for bringing him into the diocese, assigning him to a parish, and dealing with the issues that arise. Some do this extremely well, but many deal with the issues on an *ad hoc* basis, and some do little or nothing to prepare. A few priests spoke of arriving at the airport with only a parish address—there was no one to greet them or help them to find their way. One priest in Texas told us:

> I just learned about America from Hollywood
> movies. I come to this country, and it is nothing like
> the movies. It doesn't look like the cowboy movies!
> When I arrived, the culture was entirely different from
> Hollywood to where I was placed in west Texas.

The culture shock he experienced upon arrival would have been less severe if he had had something other than Hollywood westerns to help him learn about life in the United States. Another priest at that same listening session told of a recently arrived international priest who was promptly sent away to learn Spanish, before he had any opportunity to settle in and get to know his way around: "That was very disorienting. He was trying to find himself here, and all of a sudden—within two or three weeks—he is sent off to learn Spanish."

Other dioceses give the international priest a few weeks of gradual orientation to U.S. customs and culture before he is introduced to the parish.

Another Texas priest described his early experience of culture shock that was mediated by a little advance orientation with another priest:

> In my country, the priest doesn't live by himself.
> I found myself thinking what kind of life is this?
> I'm going to be by myself? After Mass, everyone
> disappears. I don't have a place to go or know anyone. I
> was so happy that someone else was there when I first
> came. Taking an international priest around, showing
> him the different places is wonderful. That should be
> praised.

One diocese has a house next to the chancery just for its international priests. The new priests live there for a month, with at least one other priest from their home country who has been in the diocese for a while. He brings them to their appointments with immigration and medical personnel, helps them fill out the necessary paperwork, teaches them how to drive in the United States, how to shop for groceries, and answers their questions about their new surroundings. They eat and pray together for this first month and gradually meet some of the other priests of the diocese. By the time they are introduced at the parish where they will be assigned, they have already recovered from the initial shock of arrival and begun to learn some of the ways of American life. Another priest, this one living in Texas, describes the acclimation process his diocese has developed as a three-stage process of integration. The first stage involves living with other priests:

> The time that they are with us—it gives them time to
> be rooted in the diocese. After some time of that initial
> human integration, then might be a good time to send
> them to a program. After a program, they appreciate
> when there are mentors to follow up. We need a
> timeline we can follow—during the different periods
> of integration.

This adjustment period for the international priest is made a little easier if the parishioners have also been prepared to receive him. They may have had little or no experience with a person from another culture. Sometimes their expectation is that the international priest will have to do all the work to fit in, as one U.S.-born priest in Oklahoma told us:

> The difficulty of coming to another country and coming in contact with another culture . . . it seems to me that our expectation is that we are the norm . . . and we expect others to adjust themselves to that norm. In parishes, there is almost no appreciation for the kind of difficulty involved in fitting into a new culture, especially for those who are already fluent in English. I've had a couple of guys tell me: "I've been speaking English for over twenty years. How can you tell me now that I'm pronouncing it wrong?" We don't have much of an appreciation for the difficulty these priests have in meeting our expectations. . . . I think that the overwhelming magnitude of change that we expect for these men goes pretty much unremarked and unappreciated in parishes.

Another priest, this one from India, told us how difficult it was for him to adjust to the realization that the parishioners at his U.S. parish have far different expectations of him than the parishioners in his home parish had.

> I am a pastor and I've faced problems with administration. We are coming from different cultures, and administering sacraments is not a typical thing. I have had some difficulty in the administration of the parish. It is totally different than in India. In India, it is a providing church—the Church provides: education, health, social, etc. The administration there is different. Here it is the other way—the people here are self-

sufficient, and the people provide to the Church. I had a good priest close by to help me work through this difference. For example: we had in India that the people are depending on us and we offer direct guidance—do this, do that. But here, we don't do that. In India, we don't have finance councils or parish councils. The priest decides everything. But here, the priest works in a collaborative way with the people. It is more complicated.

## Implication

The time devoted to preparing the international priest and the parishioners who will receive him in advance of his arrival in the United States is time well spent. A number of international priests told us that the first thing they did when they received their assignment was to search the Internet to learn what they could about their new location. The more information they have about their upcoming assignment, the better they can prepare for the transition. A vicar for clergy in Texas suggested:

> During the six months between when a priest is accepted and when he gets his visa, efforts could be made to communicate more. Visits could be made with the priest. Videos could be made and sent during that time. Intentionally use that time frame to start preparing the person to come over here to overcome the Hollywood image of the United States.

An international priest in Illinois offered this idea:

> It would be nice if the diocese had a packet prepared with some information, not just to wait until the priest is here. If they know the priest is coming, they can send it to them when they are still back in their home. Then, they can communicate any questions online. It

is a preparation that can start before they arrive. When they come, it is a continuation of the knowledge they have learned.

Another international priest in Illinois chimed in:

> The introduction before the other pastor leaves—it forms a view of continuation. The parish where I am working now, before he left, the pastor invited me a week early to the parish to get to know the people. He sent me a CD of the parish life and some literature about the parish, before I even left for the United States. When I arrived, he showed me the area and the staff, and he stayed for two weeks after that. That showed transition; the people were prepared in their minds, too. That's needed everywhere, not just in America. The passing process—from one to the other. There should be a goodbye party and a welcoming party.

Similarly, other priests mentioned that it would help incoming international priests if parishioners were prepared for their arrival. Some communication with the parish before he arrived would help prepare parishioners for their newly assigned priest. A priest in the mid-Atlantic area shared his experience:

> Parishioners need to be prepared on how to receive the international priests. In my case, the members of the parish were given a workshop preparing them to receive us. I think that could work well in other dioceses. In the archdiocese, there is a workshop that is offered to parishioners who will receive an international priest.

# IMPORTANCE OF ACCULTURATION TRAINING

Equally as important as advance preparation is some sort of acculturation training for international priests after they arrive. This acculturation process runs the gamut from an unofficial "adoption" of the priest by one or more parishioners who welcome him and help him to adjust, to a semiformal orientation and acculturation process that is organized in the diocese, to a formal acculturation training program of some duration that is conducted for priests in the diocese or offered by an external organization and to which the international priest is sent by his bishop. The way *not* to do acculturation programming was described by one priest from a diocese in the mid-Atlantic region:

> There was a priest who was met at the airport. A parishioner drove him to the parish. The parishioner said: "That is the church and the rectory—you have Mass at 6:00 a.m. Good night." That is just abuse!

An international priest serving in Illinois, who was eventually sent to the International Priest Internship (IPI) program, described his rather abrupt introduction to parish life in this way:

> From day one I started working. No one introduced me to anyone. Parishioners taught me to drive. I was plunged into the work. Until I went to the IPI program, I was pretty much on my own. There was no such help. The vicar for clergy helped me to get to the IPI program. I'm not blaming anyone, but there is no help. I was never in the U.S. before, but there was no help. I think it would be nice to have support. We don't have anybody. Some international priests have zero knowledge about this place; some of them have never been on a plane. By God's grace, I've been a couple of places, but my classmates, they haven't. It would be

really nice to help new international priests, to teach
them about the language and other information. They
have a lot to learn about America. The day I came,
there was a function for a priest, and I was there for it.

One of the issues that dioceses must tackle is the question of when to send a priest to an acculturation program. As described above, the need for a priest to minister in the parish is urgent from the day the international priest arrives, so there is pressure to place the man in a parish as quickly as possible.

A dozen or so acculturation programs exist for international priests in the United States. Some, like the programs operated by the Archdioceses of Los Angeles and Galveston-Houston, are strictly for the international priests working in that archdiocese. Others are open to international priests from around the country, such as the programs offered by the Institute for Priests and Presbyterates of Saint Meinrad Seminary and the International Priest Internship offered by Oblate School of Theology. Our survey of international priests (as presented in Chapter 3) revealed that about two in five international priests have had some sort of acculturation program, although for most of them it was a less formal program of acculturation within their diocese or religious community.

The challenge is to find the optimal time to send a priest to an acculturation program. Some suggest that this should be done early in the transition, before being assigned to a parish, because these acculturation programs typically include a module on accent reduction to help the priest with American pronunciation of English. A CARA study of international priest alumni of the International Priest Internship found that two in five had enrolled in the program within the first year after their entry to the United States. Another four in ten enrolled before the end of their second year after entry.

The training program can be disorienting, though, to a newly arrived priest, particularly if it takes place at another location and he must move there before he has the opportunity to settle into his new parish. Said one Texas priest who works with international priests in his diocese:

> So many times, we focus on how we can use them, and so we send them away to get them prepared so we can use them very quickly. We don't take enough time to share with them and teach them. That time within the diocese would be helpful.

Another timing issue involves freeing up sufficient time for the international priest to participate in an acculturation program. The men are needed in their parish assignments and arranging the time off to attend an acculturation program is often very difficult. One man, who works in an acculturation program in California, explained the challenges this way:

> The [local, university-based] program was a longer program, but the pastors and bishops said they cannot release the men. So we developed a more intense schedule. The ideal we are trying to work at is that the person who has been here long enough to know the nuts and bolts, but has questions about why people in the United States think certain ways. By focusing on what is culture and how every culture has its pluses and minuses, we have tried within the parameters that they have given us to offer something that would be helpful.

And an international priest in Illinois wondered if the time spent in an acculturation program would be time well spent:

> One of our priests has brought up the idea of an orientation program, but there is an issue of cost or time frame. If it is several months that they would be away, is it really the best use of time to have someone in a program?

## Implication

An acculturation program provides an immense benefit for an international priest, offering him accent reduction so that he can communicate more clearly with his parishioners, an introduction to the intricacies of U.S. culture, and sometimes training in particular skills, such as those related to using a computer or administering a parish. An acculturation program also provides the international priest with a little time away from his pastoral duties to focus on cross-cultural communications and other training that will help him to be more effective in his ministry. Finally, the bonds formed with other international priests who are also in the acculturation program reduce the sense of isolation many of these priests feel and increase the size of their support network.

At the same time, the benefits of an acculturation program must be weighed against the time, cost, and inconvenience of removing the international priest from his parish assignment.

## IMPORTANCE OF MENTORING, FEEDBACK, AND CONTINUING EDUCATION

The international priests that we gathered in listening sessions around the country, as well as those who responded to the survey of priests, shared a common desire to continue to learn and to improve their ministry skills. Many requested more training, ongoing formation, or access to resources such as language training in Spanish. An underlying theme that emerged repeatedly, though, was the desire for a mentor—one person, ideally a priest in active ministry himself—who would be accessible and open to questions without judging, who is experienced in the particular culture and personalities of the diocese, and who would serve as a sort of a bridge between the international priest and the diocese as he gradually adjusts to the expectations of his parish, his bishop, and the presbyterate. One priest in Texas said:

> [International priests need] a good mentor who is
> understanding and caring. That helps a lot if the
> mentor is there providing the care. Instead of finding
> fault and making fun of you, a mentor would be very
> understanding and help a lot. I would want a U.S.-
> born priest and an international priest who has gone
> through this himself.

Priests gathered in Washington, D.C., for one of the regional reflections described a mentoring program in one diocese that is designed to help international priests who are in the early stages of their acculturation. One advantage of this program is that the diocese invests resources in training the mentor so that he understands his responsibility to the international priest. Another advantage is that the international priest is expected to "shadow" the mentor for a number of months before he is assigned to his own parish:

> The mentoring program had training for mentors.
> What makes this work nicely is that when we bring a
> priest in we assign him to a mentor for six months. The
> diocese pays the cost of the priest going to that parish.
> It allows someone to come in and get acclimated
> before going to their first parish. That way, they don't
> have to depend on the parish paying for it. It allows the
> person to get their feet on the ground.

A priest mentor is ideal, whether a U.S.-born priest or an international priest who already has experience in the diocese, but some international priests do not have that option. If the diocese is unable or unwilling to provide a mentor priest, some international priests have found other ways to get the support they need. Several of them have looked for, and found, mentors within the parish in which they were assigned. Said one Texas priest:

> A mentoring parish is very valuable for what it has
> to give to an international priest. A mentoring parish
> would be a place where they don't really need an

associate, but the parish would give to the priest—
maybe he would learn about finances or religious
education programs. The mentoring parish would have
something to teach the international priest.

Another priest from Los Angeles said that, in the absence of a mentor
program, the international priest who wants to can look to a core group of
parishioners for some informal mentoring:

> A mentor program is ideal, but not always an
> option. Either that [i.e., a mentoring program] or an
> international priest—who is prepared somehow—but
> when he goes to the parish there is a core group of
> people who are involved in the parish who can review
> his homilies, and other issues.

A priest in Oklahoma mentioned the importance of mentoring as a way
of offering feedback to help them to understand their missteps and improve
their communication:

> Especially when we are pastors, it is good to have
> feedback from others. Most of the people don't tell
> us anything. Maybe we could do something about
> getting feedback so we know where we have strengths
> and weaknesses. I know that I am not perfect; I need
> to know the feedback so that I can better myself. We
> suggest that maybe there could be a process whereby
> someone would go to the parish council every other
> month and ask for feedback on the priest. It would
> be helpful for me, also. Since we are pastors, there is
> no one to give feedback; where there is an associate,
> he will give feedback, but where there is no associate,
> there is no one to offer feedback.

In addition to mentoring and feedback, many priests say the diocese needs to make sure that international priests are included in continuing education workshops offered for the presbyterate. They express strong interest in workshops and training in some very practical aspects of ministry. One international priest in Oklahoma said: "We had some [continuing education] sessions on the local diocesan policies. Later, also, we had sessions on the state policies on child abuse, women challenges, and federal laws we need to be informed about." Another priest, at the regional reflection in Washington, D.C., offered this:

> Conflict resolution—both the priest and the parish and the diocese should have skills training in addressing and resolving conflict. Not because you are international priests, but because we are human beings. Especially in the Church where people think we are supposed to love each other and never have conflict. Having the skills in place ahead of time keeps situations from getting out of hand.

## Implication

Most bishops do not have a diocesan acculturation program or other formal process for integrating international priests into U.S. culture and the culture of the diocese. Many others are reluctant to invest the time or money to send international priests to an acculturation program, even if it takes the priest away from his parish assignment for only a short time. The research suggests, though, that even in the absence of an acculturation program some sort of mentoring relationship that is put in place at the beginning and lasts throughout the first few months of an international priest's assignment can make all the difference. In dioceses that have established a mentoring process for their international priests, these priests express greater satisfaction with their adjustment to ministry in the United States and better relations with the other priests of the diocese.

One priest in Virginia describes the mentoring and feedback process that his diocese has developed in these words:

> When you come in, you are received by a priest of your home country. After three or four weeks, you are assigned to a mentor. It is a pre-assignment program. He takes you through the steps of running the parish. Now our brothers who are coming in, they are given a mentor whose duty is to help them to adjust and to understand what needs to be done in the parish. After six months, then he is assigned in a parish. . . . If a new priest comes in and is assigned to a parish without the expectations explained, the pastor will tell him what the pastor thinks is expected; but this way, they get it directly, firsthand.

Another priest in Oklahoma explains how mentoring works in his diocese:

> The mentoring program—we began at IPI. Those who arrive this year must choose a senior priest, and once a month they speak with him about priestly life. We have different sessions about this: spiritual direction and mentoring. The mentoring program is what I like—I share the activities with my mentor, and he suggests ways to live the vocation in a better way. Once a month, there is an hour of sharing with a co-priest. All alone, sometimes, we are left alone in the rectory; in India, that is not the case. Here, we feel lonely—how do you schedule your time and go about spiritual activities? Also, in India, the priest never enters the kitchen. Men never cook, especially not priests. Coming here, I cook and eat by myself. I don't know how to cook! Not even a cup of coffee. In India, every

priest has a servant. It is challenging! But, talking to a mentor helps us to understand what we are doing.

## SUPPORT FROM THE RECEIVING BISHOP AND INTEGRATION INTO THE PRESBYTERATE

Though it is hard to quantify, the support of the bishop in the receiving diocese is absolutely essential for the successful integration of international priests. Of course, no priest can minister legitimately in a diocese without first receiving faculties (official permission and recognition) from the bishop of that diocese. But beyond that, the bishop sets the tone for welcoming international priests into the diocese, into the parishes, and into the presbyterate. One priest who spoke with us at the regional reflection in Washington, D.C., shared how valued the international priests in his diocese feel because of the way they are treated by their bishop:

> The bishop knows each [international priest] by
> name. He knows where you are. He never messes up
> your name or your parish. That shows how much
> he is involved. If you meet him on any occasion, he
> remembers what you have been doing and what you
> have going on. He doesn't pause.

Another international priest—this one from Illinois—described the way his bishop makes the international priests feel welcome. In his diocese, every international priest stays at the bishop's residence for the first month, accompanying him to Masses at different parishes in the diocese and concelebrating. Once they are placed in a parish, they still meet on a regular basis with the bishop to share their experiences and discuss any problems:

> When we sit down together [with the bishop], we
> can share our experiences. It is very helpful. We have
> lunch with the bishop four times a year. And the newly

ordained are also included in this group—the majority
[of newly ordained priests] are international.

A priest from Virginia explains how the international priests in his diocese gather with the bishop every couple of months, to share information and discuss problems. He says that these gatherings help the international priests to feel less isolated:

> International priests sometimes feel isolated or left
> out. Our bishop wants us to feel comfortable; he makes
> sure that priests who come from another country don't
> feel marginalized. We meet [with the bishop] once
> every two months. We share information. In other
> areas, we meet monthly; we eat together, and we share.

Many international priests told us of bishops preparing the way for them before they began their parish assignment. In some cases, the bishop writes a letter which the pastor reads to the congregation, advising them that they will be receiving an international priest. In other cases, the bishop will make a personal visit to the parish. He might visit in advance to announce the assignment of an international priest, he might come with the international priest when he is being introduced to the parish, or he might visit the parish after the international priest has been there for a time, as a show of support for the international priest. A priest from Illinois described how his bishop visited the parish to explain his presence to the parishioners:

> I have two parishes, and I am an administrator. I was
> appointed as an administrator but authorized by the
> bishop to be the pastor. I tell the people, there are no
> other priests! So, I am your pastor, as far as the soul is
> concerned. I go to your sick. I baptize your children.
> Do not wait for anyone else, because nobody is
> coming.

It is very hard for some people. Before me was a
regular pastor, and the bishop came for a visitation
and he said: "If you see Father, you see me. I sent him,
and he is my representative. He is my other me." After
that visit, there was a clear idea for the people. And,
until the bishop pulls me out, I am here at the bishop's
will. So, I say: "Don't think there are more ordinations
coming or more priests coming, because in this
diocese, there is a lack of priests. Be contented with me,
and I will do my best to be your priest." It was a real
struggle accepting me as their administrator. During
the pastoral visit, the bishop brought some clarity
about me being the priest.

The bishop's role is just as important in ensuring that the international priests are integrated into the diocesan presbyterate. He models the welcome and acceptance that he expects of his priests. Several bishops expressed to us just how challenging it can be to bridge the cultural divide. One bishop shared this about his difficulty in getting the international priests and the U.S.-born priests to come together as one presbyterate:

The [international priests] that have already come as
ordained priests who are serving here in the diocese
have difficulty integrating, so they will all congregate
in one table or two tables [at presbyteral gatherings],
and they have difficulty mingling with the rest of the
presbyterate.

Another bishop mentioned some of the frustration that his international priests feel in trying to fit in with the diocesan presbyteral culture. They resist the implicit expectation that all the adjusting needs to come from the international priests, with no corresponding adjustment from the U.S. priests:

Last year, in our priest convocation, the international
priests said, "If you expect us to acculturate, why don't

you appreciate some of our cultures?" This has been an issue back and forth with our presbyterate about how we can appreciate also their culture.

An international priest ministering in Texas describes how critical it is for international priests to feel a sense of solidarity with the presbyterate. These priests often work in isolation from one another, and it is important that they share with their brother priests a sense of co-responsibility for the welfare of the people of the diocese:

> The input from the local clergy is important. We have heard from the parishioners, but we need priest solidarity. That is why some of us became priests. When you become a priest, you are part of a family. Your brothers are other priests. But when you come to a place where you are just there to say Mass, you are on your own. It is frightening. If something happens to you there, you have an emergency, if you don't have a connection with people, it becomes very difficult. The core responsibility of taking care of the diocese comes from the priests of the diocese. The priests are supposed to see us as their brother, as someone coming to assist them. We need to be seen as a collaborator, as someone working with their team.

## Implication

Several bishops who have long experience with international priests suggested ways to assist these priests in their transition to ministry in the United States. These suggestions ranged from more diligent preparation and communication ahead of their arrival to required participation in a formal acculturation program. Said one bishop from Texas:

> We send a form [to the international priests] before they come, and we do much more of a background

check. They have to have been a priest for at least five years and [have] five years of pastoral ministry. We ask them questions [such as] how can you relate to women and lay participation, and we ask them to write it out. We ask them to send us a tape of their voice, hopefully giving a sermon. They tell us they speak the Queen's English. I have to tell them that here in Texas we don't speak the Queen's English. We've had a few negative cases where we've had to send some people back, but in general it's good.

I think what we are finding out is we have to do much more [thorough] background checks and give them much more time just to get acculturated to where they are. We find that it's very important to give them a mentor—a priest, but also some lay people, too—to help them with basic things: where do you find the bank, where do you find the store, how we serve meals here, and things like that. Many of them want to prepare their own meals here, but often we don't have that food.

Some bishops mentioned the importance of assigning a priest mentor to the new priest, and others engage parishioners to assist the new priest:

We have our own IPF, we call it International Priest Forum. It's close to a yearlong program—intensely for two months—and then you get put in a parish, you have a mentor, and you have a group of parishioners that watch you, and it goes on and on. We have found that to be an effective way to help our international priests come to grips with acculturation issues.

Several bishops also describe the importance of deliberately including international priests in positions of leadership in the diocese. In this way, they gradually become more fully integrated in the presbyterate:

> My experience is that it takes a lot of work, but they all work well together. They really do. And occasionally one or more will be elected to serve on the presbyteral council. So we've had that for many years, and it has worked well.

> I make an effort that there be the full representation there [in the presbyteral council] of all the different groups. And not only there, in the presbyteral council, but also in the other kinds of groups, you know, with their retirement board, and with the other groups so there will be all of them active and involved.

The bishop of one mid-Atlantic diocese, who has many years of experience in bringing in and working with international priests, is very proactive in the way he integrates international priests into the presbyterate. In addition to the vicar for clergy, who is the official diocesan contact person for each of the international priests, he also has an assistant to the vicar for clergy for each of the two major sending countries from which the diocese receives its priests. These two priests, who are now incardinated in the diocese, came to the diocese originally as international priests from those sending countries and now handle most of the advance coordination and initial acculturation of international priests.

After a brief, but intense, acculturation program, the international priest is assigned to a parish for a mentorship period of six months with an experienced pastor who has already attended a program to learn how to be an effective mentor. At the end of the mentorship period, the international priest is assigned to his own parish, but he will continue to meet with his mentor for the next two years. He will also meet at least twice a year with the Assistant to the vicar for clergy for follow-up.

In addition to an annual priests' convocation, the entire presbyterate is invited to quarterly clergy study days on specific topics. Also, the vicariate meetings that occur on a monthly or a quarterly basis are another avenue for interaction among the international priests and the other priests of the region, which helps to create a sense of brotherhood among the priests who share ministry in the area.

Finally, two international priests serve on the Priest Personnel Committee, and international priests are invited and encouraged to serve on other clergy consultative committees on an equal basis with other clergy. In this way, the bishop signals to all clergy that international priests are fully engaged in all aspects of the life of the diocese.

## RELATIONSHIP BETWEEN SENDING AND RECEIVING BISHOPS

Whether the bishop has actively sought out the international priests, they have approached him for ministry, or he has inherited them from a previous bishop, he is responsible for them as long as they have faculties in his diocese. One bishop described for us how the international priests that were already serving his diocese when he became bishop have helped him to acquire more international priests. This has been a positive experience for him:

> I "inherited" Indian priests that had come from one particular diocese. That has [been a] plus, because the priests helped me with their local bishop in trying to screen priests for our area. When the priests have been involved with that, who are serving in our diocese, we have had really good priests.

An international priest at the regional reflection session in Washington, D.C., explained how important it is for the receiving bishop and the sending bishop to have a good working relationship, with open communication:

> One of the things that makes it work is that we
> have a bishop who makes it work; he loves having
> international priests. That is a gap in the research—it
> is critical the relationship between the bishop and
> the presbyterate, and also between the receiving
> and sending bishop. Our bishop sits down and does
> individual interviews with every single priest; he
> believes in international priests.

Other bishops described for us some of the pitfalls they have experienced in dealing with the bishop from a sending diocese or the major superior of a religious order who is sending priests to serve in the United States. One bishop told us that he feels as if he is getting "recycled" priests when the men are sent to his diocese to serve for just a few years. Although the religious superior in India may in good faith feel that he is sending men on mission to minister in an underserved part of the globe, the U.S. bishop is frustrated by what he perceives as a lack of commitment to the needs of his diocese:

> I think we have to make a distinction between the
> international priests who come and stay here and
> the international priests who come and are being
> "recycled," so to speak. We get them, technically, for
> four years from the Indian diocese. We have to beg to
> get them to stay one or two more years, then they go
> back. And then we get a whole new set—that is real
> difficult. Just when they are really at the peak of being
> able to administer well here, they're gone.

Another U.S. bishop feels that the sending bishop he works with is treating his priests as a commodity that he can use to barter for resources for the home diocese. At first, he asked the U.S. bishop to "tax" the salary of the international priests and send that money to the home diocese. When that suggestion was refused, he continued to explore other ways to extract assets from the U.S. bishops who have received his priests:

I find the bishop we deal with liking money. He asked
me to separate $400 from every priest's salary every
month and send it to him, and I said: "I will not do
that. I will pay every priest, just as I pay everyone else,
his stipend, and what he does with it is between you
and him." But that is the case with that bishop—I know
it's [the same thing] in [another state] and in some
other dioceses, I think, who work with that bishop,
and it's around the country, too. Then the bishop has
the audacity to visit me every year and brings me [a
small token gift from his country] and expects me to
give him $25,000 for the privilege of having his eight
priests.... But that's an issue that I deal with, and I
hear that from others, too. They may not get it, but
they put the pressure on the local diocese for that kind
of a contribution.

## Implication

As with other aspects of working with international priests, the more
structured and routinized the relationship between the sending bishop and
the receiving bishop, the better the communication between them is likely
to be. And with improved communication there is less chance of cultural
misunderstandings or the perception that one side is taking advantage of the
other. At the same time, a regularized channel of communication between
the bishops helps to lessen the likelihood that an international priest who is
deemed unfit for ministry in one diocese is picked up without scrutiny for
ministry in another diocese. This also helps to ensure that the international
priest is treated fairly, by the sending bishop as well as by the receiving bishop.

Suggested procedures for guiding the bishops and major superiors involved
in these transactions were spelled out in the booklet *Guidelines for Receiving
Pastoral Ministers in the United States*, published by the U.S. Catholic
Conference (now the U.S. Conference of Catholic Bishops) in 1999. The

document is currently under revision by the USCCB, but the guidelines have proven to be useful to bishops who consult them.

One mid-Atlantic diocese that we studied serves as a model here for good practice concerning the relationship between the sending bishop or religious superior and the receiving bishop. This bishop drafted a covenant document to guide his diocese in its relationship with bishops of sending dioceses. The vicar for clergy uses the policy guidelines established in this covenant document as a structure for the procedures he uses in working with international priests. The covenant agreement sets forth the policy of the U.S. diocese regarding its use of international priests and includes the following:

- The U.S. diocese agrees to pay a set fee to the sending diocese in exchange for the priest's service for a term of six years. The understanding is that about half of the fee is in compensation for the seminary education that the sending diocese invested in the priest, and the other half is to be used as a contribution toward the priest's retirement fund in the sending diocese.

- The U.S. bishop grants permission for the priest to serve six years in the diocese, upon completion of a thorough screening process. There is no intention for the priest to remain longer, or to anticipate incardination, unless agreed to by the sending bishop.

- The sending bishop must provide a letter of permission and an affidavit of suitability for ministry. The priest must provide four letters of reference (including at least one from another priest).

- Upon receipt of the priest's name, an international background investigation is undertaken by the U.S. diocese. The priest is also required to participate in the Virtus program of the U.S. diocese.

- Upon arrival, the priest is given a complete physical and psychological test, which is paid for by the U.S. diocese.

- The priest attends an acculturation workshop at the beginning of his ministry in the U.S. diocese, which is paid for by the U.S. diocese. The priest is also given six months of mentoring with another pastor before being assigned to a parish.

- The priest receives the normal salary and benefits given to all diocesan priests as well as the use of a diocesan car. The priest is expected to participate in all the priestly gatherings of the diocese.

- The U.S. bishop reserves the right to terminate the placement of any international priest. Upon termination, the priest is to return to his home diocese.

This policy is followed for each international priest who is accepted for service in the diocese. The covenant agreement is a safeguard for both the sending and the receiving diocese, to ensure that no one feels that priests are being "stolen" from their home diocese. It is important that both dioceses recognize that this is a temporary arrangement, for a fixed term, with the priest to return to his home diocese after his term ends. The priest is neither expected nor encouraged to incardinate in the U.S. diocese.

\*\*\*\*\*\*\*\*\*\*\*\*\*\*\*\*\*\*\*\*\*\*

We recognize that this is not the final word on the subject of international priests ministering in the United States. Their history is long and their future is as yet unwritten. It is our hope that this book serves as a snapshot not only of the history of international priests in the Catholic Church in the United States—but also and in particular of this current period when priests from other nations are "bridging the gap" in parishes around the country.

# REFERENCES

Belford, William. 2008. "Enjoying Parish/Rectory Life." *The Priest* 64 (8):30-31.

Belford, William. 2008. "Helping New and International Priests." *The Priest* 64 (7):32-33.

Budde, Michael L. 1992. *The Two Churches: Catholicism and Capitalism in the World System*. Durham, North Carolina: Duke University Press.

Bühlmann, Walbert. 1978. *The Coming of the Third Church: An Analysis of the Present and Future of the Church*. Maryknoll, New York: Orbis Books.

Carroll, John, S.J. 2008. "Letter to Propaganda Fide on Catholicism in the United States." In *American Catholic History: A Documentary Reader*, edited by M. Massa, S.J., and C. Osborn, 28-30. New York: New York University Press.

Cidade, Melissa A., and Mary L. Gautier. 2010. *International Priest Internship Participant Study: A Report for the Oblate School of Theology*. Washington, D.C.: Center for Applied Research in the Apostolate.

D'Antonio, William V., Michele Dillon, and Mary L. Gautier. 2013. *American Catholics in Transition*. Lanham, Maryland: Rowman & Littlefield.

de Brebeuf, Jean, S.J. 2008. "Instructions to the Fathers of Our Society who Shall Be Sent to the Hurons." In *American Catholic History: A Documentary Reader*, edited by M. Massa, S.J. and C. Osborn, 15-17. New York: New York University Press.

Dolan, Jay P. 1985. *The American Catholic Experience: A History from Colonial Times to the Present*. New York: Doubleday & Company, Inc.

Easterly, William, and Yaw Nyarko. 2009. "Is the Brain Drain Good for Africa?" In *Skilled Immigration Today: Prospects, Problems, and*

*Policies*, edited by J. Bhagwati and G. Hanson, 316-360. New York: Oxford University Press.

Farmer, Ferdinand, S.J. 2008. "Letter to Bernard Well, S.J." In *American Catholic History: A Documentary Reader*, edited by M. Massa, S.J., and C. Osborne, 26-28. New York: New York University Press.

Froehle, Bryan T., Mary E. Bendyna, R.S.M., and Mary L. Gautier. 1999. *Priest Personnel Profile and Diocesan Pastoral Strategies*. Washington, D.C.: Center for Applied Research in the Apostolate.

Gautier, Mary L. 2013. *Catholic Ministry Formation Enrollment: Statistical Overview for 2012-2013*. Washington, D.C.: Center for Applied Research in the Apostolate.

Gautier, Mary L., and Mary E. Bendyna. 2009. *When We Can No Longer 'Do': A Special Report on Issues in Retirement for Diocesan Priests*. Washington, D.C.: Center for Applied Research in the Apostolate.

Gautier, Mary L., and Thomas P. Gaunt, S.J. 2012. *International Priests Serving in the United States: A Report of Key Findings from the Texas Bishops' Gathering*. Washington, D.C.: Center for Applied Research in the Apostolate.

Gautier, Mary L., Paul M. Perl, and Stephen J. Fichter. 2012. *Same Call, Different Men: The Evolution of the Priesthood Since Vatican II*. Collegeville, Minnesota: The Liturgical Press.

Goodstein, Laurie. 2008. "Serving U.S. Parishes, Fathers without Borders." *New York Times*. December 28, http://www.nytimes.com/2008/12/28/us/28priest.html?pagewanted=all. Retrieved: July 19, 2012.

Government Accountability Office. 1999. "Visa Issuance: Issues Concerning the Religious Worker Visa Program: NSIAD-99-67." GAO Reports: 1.

Gray, Mark M. 2010. "In Focus: Facing a Future with Fewer Catholic Priests." *Our Sunday Visitor*, June 27.

Gray, Mark M. 2012. "Were U.S. Catholics Raptured Again?" *1964*, October 31. http://nineteensixty-four.blogspot.com/2012/10/were-us-catholics-raptured-again.html.

Henning, Richard, and Sebastian Mahfood. 2009. "Opening the Reception Process: Distance Learning and the International Priest." *Seminary Journal* 15 (2):62-68.

Hoge, Dean R. 1987. *The Future of Catholic Leadership*. Kansas City, Missouri: Sheed and Ward.

Hoge, Dean R. and Aniedi Okure. 2006. *International Priests in America: Challenges and Opportunities*. Collegeville, Minnesota: Liturgical Press.

Karoly, Lynn A., and Constantijn W. A. Panis. 2009. "Supply and Demand for Skilled Labor in the United States," In *Skilled Immigration Today: Prospects, Problems, and Policies*, edited by J. Bhagwati and G. Hanson, 15-25. New York: Oxford University Press.

Kelly, Brian. 2012. "Turning to International Priests." *The Sault Star*. July 30. http://www.saultstar.com/2012/07/30/diocese-turns-to-international-priests. Retrieved: August 2, 2012.

Mabonso Mulemfo, Mukanda. 1997. "An African Missionary in Return: Reflections on a Visit to Sweden." *Missionalia* 25 (1):100-123.

Massey, Douglas S., Joaquin Arango, Graeme Hugo, Ali Kouaouci, Adela Pellegrino, and J. Edward Taylor. 1993. "Theories of International Migration: A Review and Appraisal." *Population and Development Review* 19 (3):431-466.

Morris, Charles R. 1997. *American Catholic: The Saints and Sinners Who Built America's Most Powerful Church*. New York: Vintage Books.

Nguyen, S.V.D., vanThanh. 2011. "Who Are the 'Strangers' Behind the Pulpit?" *New Theology Review* 24 (2):81-84.

Perl, Paul M., Jennifer Z. Greely, and Mark M. Gray. 2006. "What Proportion of Adult Hispanics are Catholic? A Review of Survey Data and Methodology." *Journal for the Scientific Study of Religion* 45 (3):419-436.

Pew Forum on Religion and Public Life. 2011. *Global Christianity: A Report on the Size and Distribution of the World's Christian Population.* Washington, D.C.: Pew Research Center.

Pew Forum on Religion and Public Life. 2008. *U.S. Religious Landscape Survey: Religious Affiliation: Diverse and Dynamic.* Washington, D.C.: Pew Research Center.

Piore, Michael J. 1979. *Birds of Passage: Migrant Labor and Industrial Societies.* New York: Cambridge University Press.

Putnam, Robert. 2011. "Lost: Twenty-Somethings and the Church." Presentation given at The Curran Center and Fordham's Center on Religion and Culture, January 28, New York.

Putnam, Robert D., and David E. Campbell. 2010. *American Grace: How Religion Divides and Unites Us.* New York: Simon and Schuster.

Schoenherr, Richard A. 1993. *Full Pews and Empty Altars: Demographics of the Priest Shortage in United States Catholic Dioceses.* Madison, Wisconsin: The University of Wisconsin Press.

Schroeder, Roger. 2009. "International Priests: Different Understandings of Sexuality and Gender Roles." *New Theology Review* 22 (1):80-83.

Smith, William L. 2004. *Irish Priests in the United States: A Vanishing Subculture.* New York: University Press of America, Inc.

Sullins, D. Paul. 2002 "Empty Pews and Empty Altars." *America*, May 13.

*The Official Catholic Directory*. 2000-2013. P.J. Kenedy & Sons.

Tomko, Jozef. 2001. "Instruction on the Sending Abroad and Sojourn of Diocesan Priests from Mission Territories." Congregation for the Evangelization of Peoples, April 25. http://www.vatican.va/ roman_curia/congregations/cevang/documents/rc_con_cevang_ doc_20010612_istruzione-sacerdoti_en.html. Retrieved: July 30, 2012.

U.S. Census Bureau. 2010. Current Population Survey, Annual Social and Economic Supplement.

United States Conference of Catholic Bishops. 2003. *Guidelines for Receiving Pastoral Ministers in the United States*, Revised edition. Washington, D.C.: USCCB.

United States Conference of Catholic Bishops Secretariat of Child and Youth Protection. 2008-2012. *International Priests*. Washington, D.C.: USCCB.

University of Chicago News Office. 2007. "Looking for Satisfaction and Happiness in a Career? Start by Choosing a Job That Helps Others." Press release. Available at: http://www-news.uchicago.edu/ releases/07/070417.jobs.shtml

Wallerstein, Immanuel. 2004. *World-Systems Analysis: An Introduction*. Durham, North Carolina: Duke University Press.

# ABOUT THE AUTHORS

Mary L. Gautier (PhD 1995, Louisiana State University) is a senior research associate at the Center for Applied Research in the Apostolate (CARA) at Georgetown University in Washington, D.C. A sociologist, Mary specializes in Catholic demographic trends in the United States, manages CARA databases on Church information, and conducts demographic projects and computer-aided mapping. She also edits *The CARA Report*, a quarterly research publication, and other CARA publications. She is co-author of six books on Catholicism, most recently *American Catholics in Transition*.

Melissa A. Cidade (MA, The Catholic University of America) is a research associate and director of parish surveys at CARA. A sociologist, Melissa specializes in qualitative data collection and analysis methods as well as question development and survey design. Her work has focused on Catholic education from kindergarten through postsecondary, parish life, and young adult Catholics.

Paul M. Perl (PhD 2000, University of Notre Dame) is a research associate at CARA. A sociologist, Paul specializes in national-level polls of lay Catholics and on surveys of priests. Paul was a full-time CARA researcher from 2000 to 2005 and now works for CARA part-time while being a stay-at-home father in Pittsburgh, Pennsylvania. Paul is co-author (with Mary Gautier and Father Stephen Fichter) of *Same Call, Different Men: The Evolution of the Priesthood since Vatican II*.

Mark M. Gray (PhD 2003, University of California, Irvine) is a senior research associate and director of the CARA Catholic polls. Mark specializes in survey research, trend analysis, and cross-sectional time-series studies. A political scientist, Mark's academic research focuses on political culture, political participation, and religion and politics. He has taught courses on Introduction to the Social Sciences, Introduction to Political Science, Societal Issues, and Latino/a Culture in the United States. Mark is co-author (with Mary Gautier) of *Primary Trends, Challenge, and Outlook: A Report on Catholic Elementary Schools, 2000-2005*.

# INDEX

67, 68t; continuing formation and education, 67, 127, 129, 130; deacons, 67, 68t; integrate in the parish community, 23; lay leadership, 68t; mentoring, 23, 127-136, 137; online learning, 23; ongoing formation and classes, 68t; orientation, 23, 118, 122, 127-136, 137; parish administration and finance, 67, 68t; preaching, 23, 68t; preparation for ministry, 61-63, 118; prevalence of participation, 59, 60t, 61t, 102; recommendations for improvements, 66-67; sexuality and gender roles, 23; socialize and share experiences, 43; U.S. culture, 23, 58, 67, 68t, 90; working with women, 67, 68t; youth ministry, 67, 68t

Institute for Priests and Presbyterates, 125

*International Priests in America*, 121

IPI (see International Priest Internship Program)